A TALE
FROM
A TRAIL

Te Araroa – The Long Pathway

By Anna Grafl

ISBN 9781981035984

For you

Acknowledgements

Writing a book is like walking a trail, you don't know what you do until you finish it and afterwards it just becomes a blur. Writing about my thru-hike on New Zealand's Te Araroa Trail let me relive the journey day by day, one more time.

Also, this book wouldn't be here without the help of so many people and friends who read over my spelling mistakes a thousand times and gave me feedback on it as well as friends who helped me formatting the files. Thanks guys!

Also, a quick thanks to my family, to Mum and Dad who were happy for me to go on an adventure and especially Mum, who probably suffered from permanent anxiety attacks while I was out of cellphone reception.

A thanks to Lucie and Niko who helped me find my feet on the first day and a thank you to Davorin, Nathalie and Jocelyn.

A big thanks to my loyal Trail Family, Rick, Mike, René, Luca and Alba.

Thanks to my Kiwi family, the Hartleys, who, while writing the book had to put up with constant typing noises and a seemingly absent writer with a pale computer face.

And of course, a big thanks, for all the people out there who turned into a trail angel while helping me, whether with offering me a lift, food, a place to sleep or even just a lovely chat.

For all the ones I met during the hike and for their stories that I may have accidentally left out, you aren't forgotten.

Thru-hikers by life and family by heart.

There were so many faces and little stories that could fill a big book, I tried to keep it short and hopefully a little bit entertaining as well as maybe for one or two people out there inspiring as well.

Come on a walk with me, without getting your feet wet!

Table of Content

Cape Reinga

Kerikeri

Auckland

Te Araroa Trail

Picton

Wellington

Arthur's Pass

Queenstown

Stirling Point, Bluff

Prologue

This story is not another "self-finding-story", it is not about someone who had to make a drastic change to her life. My friends and parents are well, I didn't have super bad depression or anxiety. I may have had some minor issues – but don't we all?

There are millions of excuses out there, that stop us from going on an adventure, but let's just count the minutes and hours we spend thinking about a holiday or travelling, when we're at work, yearning for freedom and time for ourselves.
Or have you ever told someone that "one day" you would do a particular trip, but not "this year" because you "can't leave your job?"
Do we want to find excuses, or do we want to find a way to live our dreams?
I don't want to talk you into running away from very important commitments, like maybe your kids, a beloved partner or such, but always remember "where there is a will, there is a way" and I guess even compromises can be made to achieve your dreams.

I know it's easier said than done, and I, maybe too often feel too responsible for family, friends, colleagues and even bosses as well and try to make everyone happy. The question though is not whether THEY are happy but whether WE are happy. The only one you have to feel responsible for being happy is you. So, make life count with whatever adventure you are dreaming of or planning.

"One day" is not enough.
"One day" must have a date.
If you have a dream, then take a piece of paper and take a pen.

Set a date!

When I turn 26

I am 18 years old, it is a Sunday afternoon and it is raining outside. With my twin sister Julia, I am parked in front of the TV, zapping through the channels until we get caught to a documentary about people who walk 3000 kilometers on a long-distance trail, the Appalachian Trail or AT, in the USA. From Springer Mountain in Georgia over the Appalachian Mountain Ranges to Mount Kathadin in Maine.

What an inspiration: walking a distance like that, only carrying what you need and doing nothing but eating chocolates and hiking. Day in day out, for months on end. Some people do it because they need to sort things in their life, some do it for the physical challenge, some for escaping the societal rat race and some guys do it just because they want to walk.

The hikers look rugged, they look filthy and adventurous. The ones that make it the whole way completely change their look. Men grow long beards and women grow hair on their legs. They sleep in tents and share wooden shelters with mice. The only thing they talk about is their gear, the weight of the packs and food they would eat once they would hit a town after days in the wild. They look happy and content.

"This is what I want to do before I turn 26!" I say. The documentary ends, the pictures stay, and life happens.

It is 2010, I am 19 and soon I start my apprenticeship as a physiotherapist. On TV I follow the journey of Tim Cope on the documentary channel. An Australian guy who followed the route of Genghis Khan, crossing Asia and Mongolia on foot and with horses until he reaches Hungary in Europe. "This is awesome," I think "what an achievement and brave thing to do." The three-part documentary ends, the pictures stay, and life carries on. "One day."

I turn 22, it is October 2013 and I celebrate the end of my apprenticeship as a physiotherapist. But also mourn the passing of my grandma.

On TV again is Tim Cope's story about his journey across the Mongolian steppe. I watch it one more time even though I know the story.

"What a crazy thing to do!" The documentary ends, the pictures stay, and I find work in a town close to my hometown and start to earn my first own money.

"One day."

It is 2014. The work as a physio took over. It is nice working with people, but it is also hard. I don't get satisfaction out of 10-hour days with a salary where a job at a supermarket counter would bring me more. It is stressful, I partly create my own stress and then one day my body protests.

I see double images, two trees where there is only one.

We are off into hospitals, examination after examination. No real result. Being a health professional, I know what the symptoms could be, and I drive myself crazy about it. Crazy enough that I won't open my window blinds anymore, that I don't get out of bed anymore.

I stop exercising and cycling, I shut out the world, and the only time I leave the house is to go to work, but only because I must, not because I want.

I had always dreamed of travelling and of adventures but all I did was following society's rules of studying, working and following a career until my body collapsed. There were things I wanted to do and now possibly couldn't.

Back in my safe room, I mull over the possible sickness, I am 23 and my own immune system seems to shoot against my body. I may wake up one day not being able to move my legs anymore. I am 23, and I am working in a job that sometimes makes my soul bleed and that drained my energy.

I turn on the TV and there it is again: People walking 3000 kilometers on the Appalachian Trail, from Springer Mountain to Mount Kathadin.

"Wasn't that what I wanted to do?" I go online. I search for literature about long-distance trails like the Appalachian Trail, the Pacific Crest Trail or the Continental Divide Trail and of course Cheryl Strayed's book pops into my eyes. I hit the purchase button and a few days later it arrives. It's a good read. This is adventure. This is what I want.

I find Bill Bryson's book "A Walk in the Woods" and can't stop giggling "Cool thing to do, I want to do it."

I want to know more and order my first Appalachian Trail Guide. It tells me about the gear I will need, about blisters and tents. It talks about sections of the Appalachian Trail and how to prepare an attempt of a so called "Thru-hike". I am stunned and excited and can't fall asleep. As usual when bad thoughts keep me awake I visit Mum in the evenings, on the couch, just to let go and talk. But this time it is a positive thought.

I've got a plan, I've got a goal.

"Mum!" I say, "I want to hike the Appalachian Trail in the States."
"You want to do what?" she asks.
"It is 3000 kilometers, its gonna take me six months..."

"It is in the States!" she doesn't let me talk. "They have bears, the people have weapons. They have guns! I don't like the idea of you walking in forests in a land full of crazy people. Can you please just find another trail, like the Camino de Santiago, or just travel to any other safe country?!"

"The Camino?" I am gutted and disappointed "I am not 60 yet!"

Okay, I have sort of been through a little quarter life crisis with the potential illness, but it's not a midlife-crisis yet.

Still, with Mum's words in my head, I rethink.

My older sister Lina had travelled to New Zealand a few years back. She was safe. She liked it. From the Lord of the Rings I know the nature is quite nice, too.

With a little disgust over possibly having to give up the Appalachian Trail, I ask Google. My fingers slowly write the words "New Zealand" and "long-distance trail". My index presses the enter button. The screen changes:

"Te Araroa Trail!"

"Te what Trail??"

New Zealand has got a long-distance trail and it is hardly pronounceable in those early days.

"Te Araroa" is Maori for "The (TE) long Pathway (ARAROA)."

I quickly give it a read. Roughly 3000 Kilometers. Crossing North and South Island. "Adventure of a Lifetime" it says.

I close the page and have a conversation with myself; I want to do the Appalachian Trail (AT) not Te Araroa Trail (TA). But I don't want to get shot either (Thanks Mum for passing on your doubts).

"Ah for god's sake. AT or TA. It's just a swap of letters."

It is September 2014 and I start planning for Te Araroa Trail in New Zealand.

I get trekking poles for Christmas. I buy a 48l backpack as I want to try and keep it light. I get a blow up sleeping mat, a super light one-person tent, water bladders, pocket knife and clothes as well as a sleeping bag. I slowly gather everything over the next months.

Work becomes harder, I am not focused on it anymore. My focus lies on saving as much money as I can. It lies on planning a rough time schedule and going through the trail notes of the TA. The more I read and plan the more motivated I get.

Te Araroa Trail and New Zealand eventually got me hooked.

"It will be four and a half months of walking," I tell my parents.
"I will walk on beaches and forests and there are plenty of roads to follow on the North Island."
"The South Island is a bit harder and the stretches are longer, but I saw videos and it is beautiful, dangerous in places, I will have to cross rivers..."
I just can't stop talking about it.

I slowly start to tell people about my intentions and the reactions go from "You're mad!" to "Yep. Cool." from people who have no idea what I am actually planning to do. I answer the same questions for weeks and weeks.
"How long does that take you?"
Me: "Four and a half month or roughly half a year."
"All by yourself. You're a girl!?"
Me: "Yep. All by myself and yes, I am a girl. What does it matter?"
"What will you eat? Bugs??"
Me: "Unlikely. New Zealand does have supermarkets, too. I will eat normal food."
"Where will you sleep?"
Me: "I will carry a tent, there are campgrounds and hostels. New Zealand is a hiking country, so they also have huts along the way."
"Ah, so you will get a shower there and a hot meal?"
Me: "No. It is not like in the European Alps. Those huts are basic. They are like a shelter for the night not like a hotel."
"It is so risky! Are you not afraid of injuring yourself?"
Me: "Yes and no. Life is risky all the time. I could get hit by a bus while crossing the road. I do want to live my dreams and not just sit around."
"You will have to quit your job. This is dangerous and unreasonable, can you please rethink your plans?"
Me: "I will always find a job. It is not always about working and being protected by insurances in life, telling yourself that one day you are gonna live your dreams, but you never do it because you think you need to be responsible. Sometimes you must dare to jump."
"How do you carry toilet paper for four and a half months?"
Me: "Heck, no! What a question!"

I book my flights to New Zealand. October the 6th 2015 will be the day of my journey.

I sort of have all the gear and come springtime, I take leave and walk a little trek in Germany "to test my gear and prepare for the TA."
After five days I am devastated. My knees are done, my feet are covered in blisters and the little injuries take weeks to heal off. The backpack was way too small for everything and I have learned my first lesson: Always buy the gear first and then the backpack!
I order a red 58l backpack and it arrives after a few days. The bond is there straight away. "You and I, we will go on an adventure!"

I have a hard chat with my boss in April. She noticed I am not focused.
I feel sorry and in tears I tell her I want to go to New Zealand and travel.
A few days after our chat she suggests quitting in October, she would love to wait for me to come back but things and people's circumstances change, so quitting would make it clearer for both of us. I am relieved.

It is summer, and Julia and I go on a donkey hike in Burgundy in France. Yes, we were walking, no we didn't ride on the donkey! Yes, the donkey carried the gear, but so did I.

Time is flying. It is October. The last day at work. It is hard to say goodbye to clients that I had seen for over a year. I leave the practice and it is over.
I have a farewell dinner with my colleagues the day after. A farewell gift from one: six disposable undies, after she had heard that I would only carry two undies in my pack.

A few months back I met Verena, a physiotherapist herself, who found work for a while in our practice. She already lives in New Zealand and works as a Massage Therapist in Waikanae, north of Wellington.
Cool. The trail passes Waikanae.
Cool. She leaves on the same day as I do.
Cool. She will give me a lift to the airport on the 6th.

A hard goodbye to my beloved car. I will be missing it when walking.
A very hard goodbye to my friends and, in particular, my friend Katja, who I have known since 5th grade.
A hard goodbye to my older sister Lina.
A hard goodbye to my twin Julia and Dad the night before I leave.
A hard goodbye to our cat Maja.
A hard goodbye to Mum.

A hard goodbye to the house, the street, the village, the roads and familiar surroundings.

I am 24. Hello world. Hello adventure.
Here I come New Zealand and Te Araroa Trail!

With Verena, her sister and a friend of hers, we are off to Frankfurt Airport, and with the lightest luggage the check-in clerk had ever seen, yes, I left the disposable undies at home, and people asking me whether that was all I carried, I board the plane.
I will be flying to Dubai, Sydney and eventually Auckland.
Verena is flying over Asia into Wellington.
We would meet again in Waikanae, in New Zealand.

I meet a few young people on the plane. They're all 18, with my 24 years I feel old. We would have completely different experiences by the end of our travels, even though we were going to the same country.
Now, I feel a little insecure speaking English, although, I had learned it in school. Lucky me scores a seat next to a German guy, Lars. We fly from Dubai to Sydney together. For now, I am safe as the only ones that speak English are the air hostesses, the captain and a few passengers. Lars and I go the easy way and speak German.
Come Sydney, the Germans I have met and I split parts. Some stay in Australia, some carry on to New Zealand.

From the plane I see New Zealand's islands. I see the coastlines and volcanoes on the North Island.
Who would I meet on my journey?
What will it be like to set foot into another country?
Will the air smell different from the air at home?
Will my English be good enough?
I have so many questions and I am so excited.

At the Airport in Auckland I pass the customs. "Hast du Katzenzungen?" the guy asks me in German "Do you have cat tongues??"
"Katzenzungen" are German chocolate pralines. Obviously known world-wide or maybe only by a Kiwi guy that had to deal with one too many German suitcases and backpacks. "No" I quickly reply, shocked about him talking German with an English accent and I carry on.

Just before I catch the shuttle bus into Auckland I meet Lars and a few others again. We say our goodbyes. Again, our travels would be so very different.

The sun is shining in Auckland. "It is surprisingly warm for springtime." I think. It is nice seeing something new, the plants are so green, I actually feel home and welcomed straight away.
The excitement of being in Auckland leaves me shortly after. It is way too busy and loud, in the supermarkets the employees are stressed and grumpy. The hostel is dirty and full of party girls, party boys and Germans.
Where the hell was this New Zealand everyone was talking about?
Where the hell were these friendly laid-back Kiwis?
Where the hell was the nature and beauty of the country?

I had booked the hostel already in advance: Three nights for getting things ready and giving my body the chance to adjust from the jet lag.
I try to avoid most of the Germans. It is too easy to stick to them and talking our mother language rather than English. It is way too easy to get pulled into only being with them. That is not what I was here for.
With only one German girl I do a bus tour through Auckland City. I like her, but the tour I don't enjoy much. It is boring to get picked up and dropped off and not really being in the moment and the place. It makes me feel unsatisfied.
In Auckland I send a parcel with stuff I don't need now, but maybe later in the journey, ahead to Verena in Waikanae.
I have time, walk through parks and every now and then I see a little Te Araroa Trail sign on a lantern post or a tree.
This trail would become my home and this sign seemingly gave me a little warm calming hug in this busy city, and it welcomed me to the adventure of a lifetime.

I resupply in Auckland for the first stretch on the TA. I plan for five days, from Cape Reinga down 90 Mile Beach, into the small town of Ahipara.
I get mostly things I know from back home and I can't resist the high calories and the yummy Snickers bars; I could buy them "because I would be walking the length of New Zealand", I justify my purchase.

Somehow, I manage to survive the three nights in Auckland, and in the morning, I get up early to catch a bus up north and to Kaitaia. During that bus ride, which would take about three to four hours, I pass all the places

I had read about during my planning for the TA, their names are already so familiar. Outside of crazy Auckland the landscapes change from business district to houses to farmland. The surroundings just breeze by and in no time I cover a distance, that would take me weeks to walk back down again. How strange that is: Why would someone choose to do the trail and walk, rather than catch a bus or a ride?

I reach my destination and Kaitaia is so different from Auckland. Only one main road, a few shops, two supermarkets and a Warehouse. I book into a hostel and get the last bits and bobs for Te Araroa Trail and my journey through New Zealand!

Go Anna GO

It was the night of the 10th of October 2015 and the night before kicking off a dream, that I had been planning on for about a year. In less than 15 hours, I would take my first step as a long-distance hiker on New Zealand's Te Araroa Trail.

Known as "The Long Pathway" the trail crosses the length of New Zealand, 3000 kilometers, across North and South Island, leading through epic landscapes and rugged wilderness from Cape Reinga, the top of the North Island down to the Southern terminus Stirling Point, Bluff, on the South Island.

Mainstreet Lodge, my hostel in Kaitaia, was quiet and calm, there were a few young tourists, a friendly cat and a Kiwi couple, Scott and Jo, who were about to start on the same adventure as me, only a few days away.

Just before going to bed I had sorted my gear, had stuffed my few belongings into my backpack: sleeping bag inside, tent outside, everything else where ever there was space, wondering how on earth I could actually manage to carry the whole thing with three big water bottles on top. After completing this poorly attempt of looking professional and experienced, my pack was set up and ready to go.

It was cosy in the room, I had had my last shower, the heater was running, the bed was comfy, and I started to realise that by tomorrow night this comfort and safety would be gone, and I would be sleeping in my little one-person tent, together with my pack and all the stuff I had.

The alarm went off the next morning, pick up time was at 8:30am and I naively hoped to be on the trail by 11am. The transport was done by one of the tourist buses that take people all the way to Cape Reinga, and the famous lighthouse, with several stops on the way and for most of the tourists – it takes them back to their cars, accommodation, showers, hot meals, TV, WiFi, kitchens and all the amenities that civilisation has to offer.

And then, there was me, the only person on the bus with a huge and heavy pack, not knowing where she was going to end up the next nights, not knowing whether her body was going to function and now after all the doubting, whether walking and hiking was the thing I really wanted to do! Oh, how jealous I was of all those people and their clarity of the day and days. And oh, how I wasn't!

The bus trip took forever, and with every stop we had, I got more nervous; I got nervous about the time – would it be enough time to get to the first camp? Nervous because I wanted to start the trail and nervous because I couldn't stand the bus's hop on hop off ceremony that happened all the time on this tour.

Eventually by 1pm we reached our destination. The bus driver handed me my heavy pack and wished me "good luck, girl" as a woman just earlier was found dehydrated in the dunes while walking Te Araroa Trail. I gave him a very shy and quick, still German-English "Thank you" that the driver probably had heard a million times as New Zealand was like a little Germany.

In Auckland I had learned that, if you weren't careful enough, there was a German around every corner, and a comment by Kiwis "A German. Another one!" makes you realise that Germans are far away from being rare and very known in "The Land of the Long White Cloud."

I was not trying to find any Germans. Now, I wanted to get away from them.

Out on the car park I shouldered my belongings and followed the path towards the lighthouse being watched by people. Whether it was watching out of curiosity to see a person with hiking poles, or as I told myself "jealousy of this girl that was going to have adventures." I felt good. I was ready!

Taking a picture of yourself at the northern terminus of the TA is a must and it was done with another "good luck" by a girl, and I was off. It was the 11th of October and my journey began with one step at a time.

I tried to look determined and confident as I passed the people, left them behind and headed towards my first camp for the night, 10 kilometers away! It was huge!

Just one or two kilometers in I spotted two people, wearing backpacks. "Backpacks!! They must be doing the trail as well." I thought and caught up to them. Niko from France and Lucie from the Czech Republic, both having accents, like me. Perfect. They were Europeans and not German. As euro trash I felt good with them, we chatted and walked together. The two were on Te Paki Coastal Track that shares the same route with us thru-hikers for a few days. Both, Lucie and Niko loved the idea of walking Te Araroa Trail.

They were strong and faster than me and if it hadn't been for them, I probably would have gotten lost on the first day already. I had no idea what a trail sign looked like and what I actually had to follow.

It was awesome to be with them and knowing they'd be staying at the same camp in the night, gave me relief. Also, it was good to know them already and being with people I considered to be safe, especially that first night in the wild.

I puffed after them, up the colourful, yellow-orange dunes, the pack not particularly comfy on the shoulders and the feet already quite sore.

The two decided to walk a detour and I dragged myself to the last beach and up the steps to Twilight Beach Camp. Made it!

I had no bed tonight but my little tent, that I had pitched in my grandma's garden one time and once more on the short trek in Germany. I set it up, still it had not grown, I hardly fitted inside, and my pack had to remain outside in a massive blue plastic bag. Later the tent would get the name "The Coffin" but that day it was still a tent.

Not hungry but knowing I had to eat, I filled my stove with my one-liter Methylated Spirits bottle, lit it with a massive fire lighter and cooked some Uncle Ben's Rice, the flavour I knew from back home. It surely would taste – It did not and went straight down the long drop toilet, but a Snickers bar worked wonders!

A bit proud of myself, having walked and pitched the tent all by myself as well as having sort of eaten, I waited for Niko and Lucie.

In the moment when the two started to pitch their tent, I realised that I so wasn't prepared and surely was going to fail. It was a freestanding two-person temple, an easy set up just in a few minutes, spacey and robust looking, a beauty among tents. I think a bit of jealousy is healthy but that was pure envy!

In the evening we talked gear and food, like real hikers do, we talked about societal visions and politics, consumption and abundance until late in the night and I never felt more understood and home with strangers, as I did in that moment, ever before.

We said our good nights. They walked towards their beautiful portable house. I walked towards my little box.

The northern terminus of the TA, Cape Reinga

I woke up early the next morning, to my surprise not half as sore as I expected, but finding my tent soaked and wet, and the lucky neighbours having a dry tent, all ready, and set to go. Niko had decided to carry on walking the TA, whereas Lucie was going back to work, to earn money and to join him later in the journey. With a "see you later" they marched on. One can imagine them disappearing in a little dust cloud. I carried on shortly after them, with a wet tent but in good spirits.

Lucie and Niko and their palace

The track meandered through coastal scrubs and followed a dirt road towards a set of stairs, offering dramatic views onto the section ahead: 90 Mile Beach!

Ever walked on a beach for only seven kilometers? I did, it is already bloody long! This is actually 64 miles and about a 100 kilometers real length and for TA hikers that means three to four days of endless sand. Dunes to the left and sea to the right.

From the top of the stairs I spotted a big rock formation in the water and took it as a goal: "I will be there in two hours." No time! I climbed down the stairs and onto the beach. It was a fascinating feeling, this was freedom. I was set back into holiday mode, I had a beach, I had waves and sand under my feet, so much better than work.

My excitement lasted for about an hour. The views were not changing, and I was not getting anywhere close to this rock formation that I had spotted before. I realised that this could be the beginning of very long days.

I reached the last water source Te Paki stream, filtered water for the first time in my life and caught up to Lucie. We hugged, and she walked out to the car park.

I did not quite trust the filtered water from Te Paki and I didn't trust my filter to clean water from bacteria or germs yet, either. So, those two liters of water that were meant to be drunk over the next two days, I never touched, even though it was bloody hot on the beach.

The hours passed, the rock formation still in the distance ahead, I felt my feet hurting and the sun burning on my face. It felt forever, and it seemed like there was no progress at all and at the same time it was like being in a different world.

And then there it was: the moment when I finally reached the rock formation, and shortly after, the moment of trying to leave it behind and gaining distance to it again. On the beach distances were hard to capture.

There were foot prints of three people in the sand and they had walking poles, there were more people ahead than just Niko. More TA hikers.

I wondered where they were.

To make time go past I poked and broke shells with my poles and tried to test consistencies of unrecognizable washed up things on the beach.

To add a creepy experience that girls are not particularly keen on, a car drove past me, turned around, slowed down and rolled down the window. The driver slowly accompanied me for a while. He was a weird man who asked weird questions, he also looked WEIRD and offered me "a lift to a lake for a swim." I was polite and told him that, right now, I didn't want to swim and that I would walk and carry on. He drove off with an unpromising "You're crazy, girl. See you later!" and my whispering response "You're creepy and hopefully not."

90 Mile Beach is considered to be a legal highway that locals are permitted to use with their cars, to drive up and down, and to cover distance much quicker than by using the windy roads. Hence so many buses and cars.

There was a lot more poking shells and poking things, there was the excitement of waving at tourist buses as they made up their way on the beach in no time as well as confirming with my GPS that I actually covered distance when it didn't feel like that at all.

I poked more shells to distract from the heavy pain on the feet. A sudden popping blister and heavy limping left me cursing and I hoped that the day soon would come to an end.

I reached the camp site and set up my little tent, observed the damage on my feet, prepared my pocket knife for unwanted creepy "see you later" visitors in the night, and had dinner. Or not. But a Snickers bar.

The day ended with helping a French guy digging out his car that had gotten stuck in the sand. "Boy, if you would walk, this wouldn't happen to you."

Trail Journal entry for Monday, 12.10.15, Day 2

90 Mile Beach is killing me already, it is like walking in a desert. I walk and walk and walk, for hours and nothing changes, it feels like I am not getting anywhere. My feet are already sore from the hard sand.
Niko has decided to walk the TA, happy for him. He left a note in the sand for me: "Go Anna Go"

Helped a French guy digging out his car. Man, I told you, you should use the mats to get it out, not the massive branch.

Met creepy guy on the beach. Yuck!

Ground hog day two.
Beach and sand and dunes.

I didn't get weird "see you later" visitors during the night, but I surely was stiff from the 30 kilometers yesterday. Unfortunately, I noticed that the blisters had not magically disappeared over night and so I found myself hobbling along on my journey down 90 Mile Beach.
If I was lucky I would end up in Hukatere Lodge, with maybe a bed and a shower and fresh drinking water. I was close to dehydration as I didn't drink the filtered Te Paki water from the day before. The thoughts of the lodge kept me going.

The trekking poles cracked shells, tested consistencies of things, cracked shells, poked shells, tested consistencies and then it was lunchtime. Lesson I had learned so far: If not hungry, there is always room for a Snickers. Snickers rule!

I sat down on a log, unwrapped the Snickers and slowly munched on it. That was the moment when I saw glimmering shadows on the beach, debating whether it was horses or people. Surely it was horses. I sat and watched. Three people, not horses were making their way towards me and in an antisocial moment I caught myself in a thought of "If I run now, they won't catch me." I silently told myself to stop being stupid and to not try and hobble away from them. So, I sat and waited.

Happily, I waved at them once they came closer, and the three waved back. I got up from my log and we chatted.

Kiwis, nice!

Exposing me as a German. Not nice!

René, Mike and Rick, all in their 50s, for me obviously they had found a way to deal with their midlife crisis, which was escaping into a different world than offices and family life. They were sympathetic Wellingtonians doing Te Araroa Trail.

Nevertheless, I was surprised to see quite a few people on the TA.

We had a lot to talk about and a lot of regular thru-hiker questions. I got the strict ban for questions about pack weight from René's side though. "No proper TA thru-hiker talk then!" I thought. "Accepted. They won't be hearing about my awesome little light weight tent." I finished it off.

After a while I got a little lecture of "How to use trekking poles for Dummies." They had seen the sliding imprints of my poles on the beach. "You need to stick them into the ground don't slide them over the sand." Rick corrected me.

"But I get bored and it feels good."

"No, no, no, no stick them into the ground." he persisted.

The Kiwi uncles were lovely and decided to have lunch, so therefore, I continued by myself. In stronger pain, I hobbled down the beach towards Hukatere Lodge.

I poked shells, sometimes I tried to not slide the poles on the sand and caught myself sliding them, poked shells and waited for the TA attraction of the day: "Tourist-bus-waving."

The finish line was near, only a few hundred meters off the beach would be the lodge. I was in severe blister pain and in desperation of finishing that day. I think all in all I was not able to process my decisions anymore, so I walked towards the lodge, but it was not coming, way too far away!

I turned around and walked back to the beach. The Kiwis were coming, I was trapped! I quickly u-turned and acted pain free walking to the lodge with the three of them. I got a room and the Kiwis pitched their tents.

It was awesome to see Rick and René pitching the slightly bigger brothers of my little tent. If I was failing, then so were they!

In the evening I got a blister treatment by a French guy, he popped the blisters and pulled yarn through them, to dry them out, a technique he had learned in Nepal. Oh wonder! I ended up with yellow, red, blue and green yarn popping out of my feet, so I could walk a bit better than before, but still it was quite uncomfortable.

The shower at Hukatere Lodge was little but awesome. The night in the bed was great and with the next morning, out of my window, I saw the Kiwis packing up their wet tents.

They had breakfast and I, still not hungry, forced a muesli bar down my throat.

The Kiwis. Mike, René and Rick

The three started walking and I was debating whether to continue as well. I did like them somehow. I quickly packed my dry belongings in the pack and off I was, hopping over the dunes and onto the beach.

Ground Hog Day three.
Beach and sand and dunes.

After a while I caught up to the boys and we continued together. René and Mike speak a great, easy to understand English, perfect for a tourist like me. Rick was the one I just couldn't understand. I almost was afraid to walk with him by myself, afraid of not being able to understand him.
So, I walked with René and boy he could talk. Weren't men supposedly the ones that only used something like a 1000-words a day? René did like 5000 with each of us, in an hour, and on top of that he spoke some German, too. He talked about his job at the Department of Conservation, some issues that New Zealand faced with introduced animals like possums as well as his private life, which was by far too early in our trail relationship to hear about, but he seemingly didn't bother. All I had to say was "Okay" and "Oh" and he seemed happy with it.
He had also walked the Camino de Santiago with his oldest son a few years back. "Ha!" I thought, reassured in my theory: "A midlife-crisis!"

We had to leave the beach because of high tide. They lifted me up the banks and we walked on a parallel forestry road towards our next stop. The first time I encountered 10 dumped microwaves, fridges and old ovens on the side of a track. "That much about 100% pure New Zealand!" the Kiwis commented briefly and cynically on New Zealand's tourism advertising slogan.
They seemed much fitter and less munted (Kiwi slang for hurting/ broken), so by the time we reached Waipapakauri Holiday Park they only had lunch and carried on to Ahipara, whereas I decided to enjoy the amenities of civilisation again, and to break up the last stretch into halves. Wimp I was! I only had started a few days ago and already enjoyed the comfort of a roof rather than my little box. Where would that end?
I lifted my legs and got the weight off them, still not hungry for proper dinner, I had another chocolate bar and went to sleep.

Another morning and a new day, my feet were still sore but a tiny bit better and even packing the backpack was easier now. My tent went on the outside, sleeping bag in the bottom, cooker and mat halfway, clothes on top and then the food.

Ahipara was about 14kms away and so I wanted to be there around lunchtime.

I hit the beach.

Ground Hog Day four.

Beach and sand and dunes.

I poked shells, slid the trekking poles, thought of the Kiwi-lesson and corrected the poles-walk again. I poked more things and dragged myself towards the little township of Ahipara.

Again, the distances on the beach were hard to get: I could see Ahipara and the end of 90 Mile Beach for a long time already, but it felt like I was hardly making any progress in getting there, hours went by, and then finally I reached my destination.

There were people on the beach, cars on the beach and the access to town with the last meters to the hostel.

I had a warm welcome from René, who grabbed the pack off my shoulders and gave me my first TA hug.

The Kiwis shared a cabin, I got a bed in a dorm and had a shower with the last of the shower gel, Mum had given me. I smelled good and it lasted for the hand wash of my clothes as well. Clean and content, satisfied with the first achievement on the trail, I even had my first proper pasta dinner after almost five days!

Rick, René and Mike had already had their Zero Day, a day of not walking, a rest day, and they would be carrying on tomorrow morning, onto the forest section. The three had 141 days for doing the TA and had created a proper time schedule for the trip. Therefore, from day one onward they knew how long they had to walk each day, and where they had to end up in the evening to make sure to get to Bluff on the 28th of February 2016. Rick was the one that had to be back at work in March.

I had read that the forest section was a hard test, as the forests (Herekino, Raetea, Puketi) were dense, super muddy, and there were proper trail markers to follow (90 Mile Beach was easy to follow, even I didn't get lost). Egoistically I loved the idea of joining them and had a quick resupply in the little store in town.

Came the next morning I could not join. The blisters had gotten worse over night, they burned and looked red, were painful to walk on. I said my goodbyes to the team, gutted as for whatever reason it felt right joining them, now being left by myself again. Hugs and a not serious "See you in Mangamuka Bridge." from René and they were off, leaving me thinking "Surely not!"

Still disappointed with the whole thing, I was lying in my bed, worrying about the blisters, worrying about the journey, me alone in the woods, worrying about not seeing the group again.

Later at the reception, the hostel owner handed me a plastic bag with two left-behind towels and a note "Mike, René and Rick."

"Awesome!" I thought, and I started to worry about whether to skip a section on my adventure already and to return the towels to their owners and to join. With that I would agree to their TA schedule and I would sacrifice my trail freedom for the chance to be with those awesome people. Was it the right thing to do?

A Swiss girl gave me a lift into Kaitaia to see the doctors. From the hospital I got advised to go and see a General Practitioner, fair enough, I was not dying; blisters are obviously not a good enough reason to go into a hospital for. I then hobbled through Kaitaia to get my antibiotics from the GP. It was a great result on the TA; I had walked five days, already had infected blisters and already had one visit at the doctors. On top of that, I had lost the Kiwi group, of course I didn't feel pumped that day.

I comforted myself with a fizzy drink and chips from the supermarket as well as bought a little "Trail Symbol" that I had spotted on the Kiwis' backpacks. It was a Jandal Key Ring.

For those who wonder "What the heck is a Jandal?!" A Jandal, or "Japanese Sandal" is the Kiwi expression for the German word "Flipflop" or the Australian word "Thongs". Jandals are an unofficial national symbol for the Kiwi lifestyle. Some Kiwis would even wear them in winter.

If one ever wants to be a proper Kiwi, one must own a pair of Jandals!

The challenge of getting a lift back to Ahipara meant "thumbs out" and hitchhiking. For the first time in my life. And boy, we learn a lot when we do things for the first time.

Not quite ready for standing on the side of the road, I frantically ran around on the supermarket car park, asking friendly looking people whether they were on the way to Ahipara. I got plenty of "Nos" and a tip to write a sign for the hitchhike. Said and done. The road was waiting, and the sign worked wonders. Lucky me scored a lift with a super friendly Maori woman, and the best: her, her foster son and husband would be off to Kerikeri tomorrow! If I needed a lift there too, she asked.

"Yes! Yes, I do." I said and with that I had made my choice to catch the Crew!

The woman dropped me off at the hostel.

I discussed my plans with Nathalie, a Belgian woman, who had just arrived from Cape Reinga. She was doing the TA as well. She told me not to run after people, but to do my own thing instead and to leave the towels behind.

But the next morning at 7:30am, on time, the whole family and I were on the way to Kerikeri. We drove past the Herekino, Raetea and Puketi Forests, all three covered in clouds and mist. "Shouldn't I be walking that instead of rushing by in a car?" I did feel disappointed, but it also felt so right to try and make it to Mangamuka Bridge and to join the group.

On the way, the little son had a swimming lesson in a pool and I was allowed to join and watch. I felt grateful to be able to watch it and to get the chance to be with this lovely family.

The husband, a teacher for Maori language sent me off in Kerikeri with a little Maori blessing. Safe travels!

It was early in the day, and if I was lucky with the lifts, I could reach Mangamuka Bridge in the afternoon. After a quick resupply and as I had learned, I wrote my sign.

Again, I was lucky. The first lift took me out of town, the second took me into the middle of nowhere, and the third took me to Mangamuka Bridge. Mangamuka Bridge is not much, a small settlement along State Highway 1 between the forests. It has farm houses, plenty of fences, dairy cows, an old radio station, a dairy store (A Deli or corner store) and public toilets. That's about it.

TA generosity awaited me from the owner and good soul of the dairy store who offered me to pitch the tent in her garden. The trail provided:

I had had no idea where to stay that night and suddenly I could pitch the tent in someone's backyard. I noticed that after having been on my New Zealand adventure for about a week, I actually almost found it exciting now not to know what was happening next. I got that belief that something good would always pop up, and more or less stopped worrying about it.

I pitched my little tent with support from Gingernut, a ginger cat that found it very interesting and fun to play with tent walls and strings, in particular when there was wind and rustling noises involved. Imagine, lying in your little tent and suddenly you have a cat jumping in your back and crawling into the tent.

I dearly love cats, but when the only house you have is the one that just got destroyed by four paws and a mouth full of little teeth, it crosses the line, so I found a way to distract the naughty puss from my shelter.

In the night, two more hikers turned up. Rebecca and Jonny from England, a lovely couple, with this awesome tent that Niko and Lucie had – again – I felt under prepared and small in my little box.

The next morning by the little dairy along the highway in the middle of nowhere was a slow one, I had breakfast in front of the dairy, told myself that today the Kiwis would turn up, I sat, and I sat, and nothing happened. I talked to Rebecca and Jonny, they were fed up with the forests. It was hard and long days, not much fun for them, so it must have been the same for my three Kiwis.

Every 15 minutes a car drove by on the road, a few stopped at the dairy, a few stopped for the toilets. A day on State Highway 1 can be a long day, too, and not much fun either.

Then there was another hiker coming towards the store. Luca, from Italy, he loved the forests. Rebecca, Jonny and I guessed he must be a bit crazy. While the four of us had a chat, a car pulled over and out got a small man, almost Hobbit-sized with red hair and a shirt with a statement we all could easily rely to "Not all those who wander are lost." It sounded familiar and he looked familiar. His name is Geoff Chapple, he is the father of Te Araroa Trail and he is the guy that made it possible for all of us to enjoy the journey. He was fun and interested in our hike, he knew how it was, to be on the trail and wished us all the best and happy hiking.

He must be so proud, seeing people following his dream and getting out there on an adventure!

Luca, Geoff Chapple, and Rebecca and Jonny in front of the dairy

In the early afternoon, Rebecca and Jonny got a lift to the next forest section and Luca remained with me. He was good to talk to and again, like with all the hikers so far, there was a special bond, something that made me feel home and being understood. We spent hours sitting by the side of the road at the picnic table and watched cars going by.

With an afternoon beer from a drunken motorcyclist and fresh pancakes with butter and jam, homemade by the dairy owner, time went by and the evening came. I shifted from my tent into "the nest", a little room with a bed next to the dairy, and Luca and me, both, had dinner with our host and her daughters. No Kiwis that day!

It rained overnight. In the morning Luca and I decided to wait for the group just a little bit longer and if they wouldn't turn up, then we would head off by ourselves. But what a surprise: Niko was the first to arrive, he got a big hug and the Kiwis were not far either.

Hugs from all, they had experienced massive days in the forests. I handed them their towels, they had breakfast at the dairy store and then we started onto the next section. Niko, Luca, René, Rick, Mike and I with Jonny's muddy trousers, that he had accidentally left behind - Seemed like I had found my role on the trail: Gear Donkey!

The Fellowship of the Trail

It was awesome to be with the team. Again, it felt right and familiar walking with these people.

The days in Puketi Forest were mind blowing for me. River routes were to take, which means you don't have a proper track given to you to follow, but instead you must pick your own route through it.
The water of the rivers and streams was clear, the deep green colours of the bush were remarkable, as were the ferns and trees, and the sound of foreign birds made me think of broken stereo boxes.

We passed stands of giant mature Kauri Trees that had survived the early gum diggers: In the 1830s, workers had come into the Northland region to take off the gum that was attached to the bark of Kauris and sometimes it was found on the crown of the trees as well. In that process they would cut down the trees that had grown for over hundred thousand years, take away the gum and leave the wood to itself, to either rot or sometimes they would just burn it. Those trees we passed in Puketi had survived this massacre when they were babies. They were probably only a third of the size a Kauri could get.
Look at me, how lucky I was to be able to experience that. I could have been at work, like every other day, but not now, my feet were wet, the wind was blowing through my hair and the sun was on my face.
This day was my first proper "Kiwi tramp". I still had to find my feet, but only slipped once on a muddy and slippery track, almost ending up with a broken arm.

We would sleep at Puketi DOC Campground that night, René had gotten us the bookable hut there, for free. We ascended to the campground on a forestry road and us, we three European youngsters, had the joy of being introduced to the Department of Conservation's pest control; along the way, on almost every third tree, they had installed possum traps.
Possums were introduced by the early settlers in the 19th century, as with their thick and soft fur they seemed to be just made for the "fur industry". Sadly, some possums escaped their destiny and happily bred and lived of native plants as well as birds. In Australia, possums are protected. In New

Zealand, possums are predators to birds and bush. But their processed fur is welcomed in combination with merino wool and eventually in cosy and warm scarfs, gloves or beanies.

In Puketi Forest, the possum traps sat about a meter above the ground and every single one of them seemed to be successfully killing these fluffy, furry animals, as their bodies except for the heads, dangled off them. The air smelled of rotten bodies. I figure as a DOC guy the smell was a treat to René's nose. "Hhhhmmmm, the smell of success!"

In the morning we left the campground and walked towards Kerikeri and a Zero Day. Once there we booked a cabin for all of us, beds, roof, showers and afterwards we went out for dinner to a pizza restaurant with Luca's attempt to teach a Kiwi how to pronounce "Pizza Funghi" properly, which made us all laugh.

"It's not fuuuaaaanghaaaay" he said.

"It is 'Funghi'!" he corrected with his Italian accent and both his hands, with the fingers bunched together and the tips touching and pointing upwards, would form the famous Italian gesture.

"We don't say muuuaaaashroooam" he continued.

"We say 'mushroom'!" and both his hands would do the gesture again - but this time, adding to the up and down movements of his wrists, the arms waved threatening as well.

A Zero Day always means sleeping in, lying in, no unnecessary walking, except for purchasing food in cafes or supermarkets, and lots of eating. One would do the resupply for the next section of the trail, as well as sometimes gear shopping to replace broken things or maybe get something different that would hopefully work better. For me it was time to get new boots. The old ones, from Germany were munting my feet and the blisters were still not forgotten. I fell in love with a pair of boots that fit my gaiters and on top of that I bought new socks. What a day.

I think Zero Days are, like back in school, when someone asked you about your favourite topic and you would answer "the breaks", one of the best parts of thru-hiking. Nothing is more rewarding than hitting a town after having spent days on end in the wild. All the showers feel fantastic and one could really feel how clean a body could be after the wash.

Also, Zero Days usually mean hitting civilisation, traffic and noise. In the bush of course you didn't see cars, zebra crossings, or traffic lights. In the bush you didn't need to wait in a queue at the counter or look from right to left or left to right while crossing a street, or in the bush, a road would be a stream.

In Kerikeri, René supplied us European youngsters with our very own Trail Jandal Key Rings. The three of them already had the unofficial New Zealand national symbol dangling from their packs, gifted by a friend. So, he decided to carry on the tradition, as "Trail Jandals couldn't be purchased for yourself, but had to be a present from someone."

I handed the one I had bought in Kaitaia to Niko and Luca and I got ours from René.

After Zero'ing in Kerikeri we carried on along New Zealand's Hibiscus Coast, down to Paihia, crossed the Waikare Inlet by boat in the early morning hours, walked in a stream and on a lovely track for most of the day. Then we hit a road for the last kilometers to Oakura and eventually munted our feet on the tarseal (Kiwi for "concrete road"). That night we ended up on a campground just before Helena Bay, it had started to rain earlier in the day and it was still pouring, while we all sat under the roof by the campground's kitchen, debating whether to put up our tents or not. I knew if I would try to pitch my tent in the rain it would be soaked within a minute and so I prayed that the Kiwis were stubborn, too and that we might get the chance to sleep under the roof. Niko had his palace tent already up and perfectly dry. We all were jealous.

The boys however had found the perfect way to avoid pitching the tents. A big blue Tarpaulin was the answer. In less than 15 Minutes they had built our shelter for the night. One could tell that it was not the first time they had done it, and all agreed it reminded them of tramping trips with their kids, when they were younger.

It was perfectly dry underneath the tarp and once we all had snuggled in our sleeping bags, lying next to each other, it was a cosy night. Also, I was surrounded by the best Kiwis in the world.

Niko left us the following day while walking into Whananaki. He decided to have longer days and get more kilometers in, before Lucie would join him in a few weeks' time.

When we got to Whananaki's campground Niko had bought every one of us an ice cream and the camp owner handed us a note, he had left us. Niko had loved walking with the team and we would see him again on Whanganui River. Au Revoir Petit Général! Au Revoir!

Now we were five people left.

We all reached Ngunguru (potentially pronounced "Nanaruu", we had no idea how it was pronounced and neither did some Kiwis) in the early evening. Our feet were sore from the road walks that day and the days before, and we desperately needed to stop. I checked my trail notes and found two campgrounds listed on the map. We were dreaming of a little cabin to squeeze in, a hot shower, and just a roof over our heads, especially as we had another Zero Day planned the next day.

It turned out neither of the camps existed anymore, so we ended up at a local's place who sometimes let campers stay in the backyard. Instead of a cabin, we pitched the tents but still we had a warm shower each.

After we had tortured our feet on the roads in the last days, none of us felt up for the next section which would have involved more than 20 kilometers of pure road walking as well as a climb over a hill and down towards Ocean Beach. We found a brochure about sea kayaking: What a tempting thought that was; we would still follow the trail with our own stamina and muscles, but instead of tarseal, we would have kayaks in the water. Everyone was happy with the plan and we called the operator.

After having had our Zero Day we met up with Mark who would kayak-guide us along the coast to a beach before the last hill, so we only would have to quickly pop over it and we would reach our destination.

We paddled in our kayaks along the coastline, had a few stops and a great lunch along the way and eventually got out of our boats.

Me, with wet shorts and wet shirt, the Crew dry as a bone.

I must have done something right there. Not.

All we wanted that day was a good place to stay for the night. We kept fantasising about a hut with a roof or a shed. We would take anything to avoid pitching our tents. By now, René and Rick had realised their tents were like mine: they were coffins or like René used to call his tent an "Emergency Shelter."

Our wishes must have been heard that day. We found a big wooden beach shelter with a bar, a table and chairs, it even had electricity. Quickly we walked to a house nearby to ask for permission to stay. The owners of the beach bar happily agreed, and the decision was made: No one would pitch their tents tonight.

It was perfect, especially as this shelter was so close to the river mouth that we had to ford in the early morning. The river runs into the sea and therefore it was tidal, so we had to catch it at its lowest to make it an easy crossing and had to get up quite early.

In the early hours of dawn, a grumpy Mike admonished us to get going and pack, as we kept mucking around and took our time to get sorted. It was already way later than we had planned to ford the river, but no one seemed to rush except for Mike. He took off without us, angrily mumbling to himself and we could see him a few minutes later almost being swallowed by the waves of the sea and the river. We had waited for too long; the tides had turned, and the water was already coming back in. Luca, René and Rick crossed the river at hip depth. I was the one to be left behind. I feared fording the river where they had crossed and tried to find my way further upstream. I told myself that the water would be lower there.

For whatever reason, I had never done it before, and maybe it was the fact that the water was salty and sandy, I made the worst mistake and a typical European thing: I had decided to take off my boots! I stepped in the water with bare feet. That turned out to be my lesson for the day and for the next time to definitely keep my shoes on. While crossing, I couldn't see the ground underneath my feet and I didn't think of the sharp mussels that were hiding in the sludge. Their sharp ends cut wounds into both my poor feet and the saltwater straight away made them burn. Still I fought against the incoming tide and the highest the water got during the ford was up to my hip belt. On the other side I walked sand into my cuts and it took me ages to get my feet cleaned.

The first hours after the mussel incident I walked like on sharp shards.

I had learned my lesson and René took the piss, when he invented my "Liebe Mutti Moment."

"Dearest Mum…, Liebe Mutti…" he said and continued on like he was writing a letter to Mum about my "(mis-)adventures". From now on, whenever there was a ridiculously insane TA action on the track he would briefly comment it with "Liebe Mutti…" and it always made us laugh. Sorry Mum, while we took the piss, I have to say some of those moments were actually really creepy.

Just shortly after everyone had made it to the other side of the river it started to drizzle and all in all the forecast for the day seemed rather wet than dry. We carried on, followed Ocean Beach until we got the next "Liebe Mutti Moment" when we hit a big sandy, rocky cliff, that grew steeply for about 10 meters and of course it was part of the trail.

There were only a few roots and rocks to hold on to and it made me realise that everything was possible on the TA. I obviously had chosen a trail that was not just a hiking trail, but a rock climbing, almost swimming, bush bashing and boulder hopping one.

In fact, that is exactly what Te Araroa is: Kiwis are not just hikers, they are trampers.

Tramping is for hard core hikers and usually it involves more moves than just stepping on foot ahead of the other. Tramping is a full body workout!

And then it poured down with big, heavy raindrops and we were soaked in minutes. There was a settlement at the end of the beach and what was even better were the public toilets close by. Rick, Luca, René and I, together with our four bulky packs, managed to squeeze in the men's, to have a snack in the dry. It didn't make much difference, to be fair, the rain didn't change in those minutes and it wouldn't. We had to leave the toilets and climb up Bream Head ahead of us. The track climbed for about 450 meters above sea level, everyone was wet and after having crossed the river in the early morning, the beach walk and the dune climb, we all just felt tired.

The one that always kept us going was René. I remember him on Bream Head, descending a slippery rock part, while singing with his loudest voice that burst me into laughing. René is chatty and cheerful. Of the three of them, he was the one who definitely always saw the positive side of things. If something wasn't positive enough, he would take the piss out of it, and sometimes in those moments it was hard not to wet yourself laughing. René was from the beginning on a joy to walk with and for me, especially as always in doubt of not knowing what to talk about and worried about awkward breaks in chats, a chat partner in crime.

Bream Head, covered in clouds and in the rain however was a beautifully spooky atmosphere. There was no view from the summit and the tracks were slippery, but what made it unforgettable were all the plants, that with the rain looked sparkly and shining, the green of the ferns was even richer than before and already we agreed, it was a day to remember.

Poor Mike wasn't quite as happy with the outcome of the day, he had slipped and fallen numerous times on the wooden and wet stairs on the way downhill and had hurt his back.

We stayed in a beautiful Bed and Breakfast in Urquarth's Bay that night, where Luca cooked us a lovely Italian risotto that we shared with our hosts. Just before bed time I hopped under the shower, examined my injured feet and squeezed out a little black mussel from underneath my skin. The day of the mussel incident had ended.

To get to Marsden Point the trail notes advised hikers to look out for boats or sailors to catch a ride over the estuary. With five people in our team, we considered our chances as fairly low to get us across together. Therefore, we had already called a guy that offered us a lift. Expensive at NZ$40 each and eight minutes later we reached Marsden Point, a big oil refinery. Again, the sun didn't shine for us in the morning. With the big dark buildings and the massive pipes of the refinery it made the whole area rather depressing than joyful. The one big delight for us hikers was the Marsden Point Canteen where each of us purchased a second breakfast. Apparently, the food gave us enough energy to make a good pace after. We walked through Ruakaka and later switched to Uretiti Beach along Bream Bay where the track then turned off onto a road and into Waipu.

Here is a big pro when you walk with Kiwis:
They always know someone, somewhere!

In this case it was Rick's family. Pat and Claire live in a rural area out of Waipu and the two picked us up soon after we had left the town. Pat works as a Naturopath or as I called her: "Herb Witch" in a little studio in their backyard which turned into my room for the night.
Claire is fascinated by subtropical plants, grows them and sends them off to people that bought them.
Their place is beautiful and is filled with a good spirit and love.
Both of them apologised for not having a shower installed yet, we would have to have a bath each. Oh bummer! The massive windows in the bathroom gave one the chance to enjoy the views while soaking in the hot water. One could see over the hills, over Waipu, the beach, Ruakaka as well as Marsden Point and all the way in the distance Bream Head.
Pat and Claire also made us a wonderful dinner and a lovely breakfast the next morning.
They dropped us off, except for Mike whose back was still hurting, where they had met us the day before and we walked on the road without our packs. We met again a few kilometers further on a car park and the entry into the forest. Mike and the packs were waiting for us, and from there we followed the track markers into Mangawhai Heads.
We entered bush and crossed farmland over green rolling hills and little valleys and that day we got spoiled with the most amazing coast views. Still all the way the trail provided us with little and big surprises, people's

generosity and support was just amazing, even for a big group of smelly hikers.

In Mangawhai Heads we had planned another Zero Day, so we checked into "The Coastal Cow" hostel where we then got a freshly baked carrot cake from the hostel owner with an apology that the icing was a bit runny as the cake was still warm. Wow – We so didn't care.

We started our Zero Day with an early get up in the middle of the night to watch the Rugby World Championship final, New Zealand against Australia. In the rivalry between Aussie and Aotearoa that match was the most important ever. With that being my first ever Rugby match I didn't get one single rule of the game, so I just sat there watched those half naked men rushing into each other, forming meatballs on the ground to get the ball and most importantly, I made sure that my 50-year-old Kiwi uncles didn't die of a heart attack when eventually their 'All Blacks' scored the trophy.

After this exciting event I went for a walk and scored another wonderful freshly baked cake, that I got gifted when a woman on the road, Glenyce, picked me up on my little stroll and took me home. She ran her own cake shop but hated eating cake. "They made me fat!" she said and pointed out that she had already lost 63kg after she had stopped eating them.

We hikers didn't bother with weight issues and loved her cakes as much as we loved the carrot cake!

In Mangawhai I had finished mulling over my small tent. After hesitating and refusing to put up my coffin every night the last weeks, I decided to get a new tent as soon as we would hit Auckland. And for sure by tomorrow, I would send Jonny his muddy trousers that he had left behind in Mangamuka Bridge!

Until Mangawhai we hadn't met any other Te Araroa hikers and were already wondering where everyone was and then finally we met four other hikers the next day; a Belgian guy that dragged a German along as well as an American guy that dragged his partner along, the two had just gotten married, and the TA was their honeymoon, so therefore he forced her to do 40 kilometers a day and we all agreed that she did not quite look happy after all.

Again, we followed the coast and ended up on beautiful Pakiri Beach. It was a lovely warm day and the boys, except for Mike, decided to go for a swim in the sea. Off came the clothes and three naked bums disappeared in the water while Mike could only shake his head in grumpy disbelief and hid his eyes.

Mike was the one that always seemed a little more serious on the journey and in a conversation. He is René's older brother and being the eldest of three, he probably always was the responsible one, the caring one, the one that looked after his brothers when they were younger. Nevertheless, he is also the one with a great sense of awareness and notices every little flower or bird along the track. He was the happiest person in the bush but never on the roads. Whenever we took a step on tarseal he would sing, with his deep voice, his little mantra "Hello darkness my old friend, I've come to walk on you again." and march on in resignation.

That day, I swam too, but kept my clothes on. "You got to wash off the salt or you will get chafing" I got the lecture of my uncles, and off they were into a stream close by, to frantically wash their bodies. Later they learned that the water they had used to wash off the sea salt, actually was salty, too. After filtering water from the stream no one had tasted it until dinner time. What was perfect for cooking my couscous with, was not quite the best for a lovely cup of berry tea for my Kiwis. We live and learn, don't we?

The five backpacks

Again, it was Rick's family who welcomed us after a super long day on the beach and in the bush the next evening, when they picked us up from Govan Wilson Road. His sister Gaye and her family hosted us for two nights in a row, which made it easy for us, as we could walk without our packs the next day. Rick was the only one to carry a pack and he was happy for everyone to put their water bottles and important gear in it. Whenever Rick could help, he was there, for everyone. He probably was the 'sweetie' in the team, always pleasant, genuinely positive, always happy with whatever decision we made and never in a bad mood. He truly has the gentlest soul and character.

Rick made it his job to teach us Europeans and show us how to tramp, how to cross rivers safely, and he showed us all the native plants New Zealand has to offer. He actually really enjoyed it and us. Sometimes we just loved to call him Rick Grylls, after the outdoor champ Bear Grylls. Rick had done kids scouting in the Hutt Valley near Wellington for many years. He educated the children to be prepared in the bush and it was an excellent balance to his job in the office. And after having walked with Rick for quite a while now, I even got to understand his Kiwi accent better and better; no longer was I afraid of walking with him.

Without our packs we were even quicker on the tracks, reached the Dome Cafe and nearly stripped it for their food, we had become very, very hungry TA hikers and no muffin, quiche, pie, ice cream, cake or hot or cold drinks were safe.

Gaye's husband Paul picked us up again once we reached Matthew Road a few hours after the big feast. For us four it had been an awesome day, not so much for Mike though, who hadn't joined us for today's walk. His back was still very sore and kept him from walking. He got a lift into Puhoi the very next day, while we followed the trail and later caught up with him again.

Once in Puhoi the hiker hunger had captured us again and we robbed the little general store with its baked treats and drinks.

Rob Wakelin, the Te Araroa CEO (Chief Executive Officer), had made contact with René. Due to René's online blog and link with the Department of Conservation Rob was interested in his views on the trail.

After Luca and I had met Geoff Chapple in Mangamuka Bridge, we were now to meet the most important person for the TA Trust.

Rob was a lovely guy, he was interested in the Crew and especially enjoyed the boys' stories of the Northland Forests. After he had listened to René's, Mike's and Rick's version of how beautiful the forests were but also how muddy and hard it had been, he burst into laughter, when Luca told him that he absolutely loved it in this green hell, that sometimes forces people off track and eventually to end their TA journey due to traumatising experiences.

I didn't have any stories about the first forests, which briefly made me sad and I had a little regret about it and the towel incident. It didn't last long that very moment. More importantly now was that we all were still together.

Rob took pictures of us and we took pictures of him with us. He stayed in contact with René even after finishing the trail and was a great initiator for Te Araroa Trail. Rob Wakelin finished his work as the CEO in March 2018.

Rob Wakelin, René and Rick in Puhoi

When the TA got officially opened in 2011, many sections, that we had experienced in our season, hadn't been part of the track then. One of them was the section from Puhoi to Wenderholm Estuary. Originally hikers were supposed to take another tarseal road but due to roadworks a few years ago the TA Trust diverted the trail onto Puhoi River. That did not just make a kayak operator happy, but also our feet. We spent the afternoon, glamorously relaxed in single kayaks, while following the river down the estuary. We all loved it and I know there are a few people that say it is too expensive and one should walk a long-distance trail rather than kayaking it – well, I speak for all five people in our group – none of us would want to miss out on this beautiful time on Puhoi River. That is what makes the TA so different from other long-distance trails. Where else would one walk on a beach, in the bush and paddle a kayak in one and the same day? That is only possible on Te Araroa Trail and if there are locals, like dairy store owners, tour operators or just any kind of shops, that benefit from us walking tourists, then we may as well leave some money there. For the good people, that are happy to help us out and always have an open ear for our trail stories.

After the paddle we pitched our tents by the estuary and with the Guy Fawkes fireworks on the 5th of November we glazed into the starry sky. We were at peace and I was at peace with the trail and my friends. We had had a great time in Northland. I enjoyed being with this team. Loved them all to bits, I loved how different they all were and what an important part they now played in my daily life. I had found friends on the other side of the world. We had made our first footsteps on the trail together and already we had become a little Trail Family.

The team by the Wenderholm Estuary

Trail Journal entry for Thursday 5.11.15, Day 26

We left Gaye and Paul this morning to walk towards Puhoi.
Walked through bush and farmland, it was a wonderful walk, especially walking into Puhoi.

Had food and drinks while talking to Rob Wakelin the TA CEO, lovely guy.
Solo kayaked until Wenderholm Estuary! WOW. I loved it.
I love kayaking. So nice to see I can do it and even after having developed into a "land person" I can actually be a "sea person" too.
It was just so relaxing.
The team had a lovely evening by the estuary, pitched our tents were we probably are not allowed to, no one cared, I funnily enough don't care.
It's great to have the four around me, they all are super lovely, and it feels like they care for each other and us. Love them!

Fireworks for us tonight.

Happy Birthday, Papa!

Crossroads

Northland went by and Auckland was to hit us with five days of road walking. From a small camp in Stillwater, we had to cross a tidal estuary and with a little help by Rick, I managed to carry my pack above the head to the other side without drowning.

Then we hit the north shore of Auckland. We passed packed suburbs with posh cars, and massive houses, with perfectly mown lawns, all of them surrounded by big fences or hedges to keep unwanted visitors away, and to keep their privacy. The number of people that we passed now was probably double the number of humans we had encountered in the last weeks further north. From a friendly, hospitable and welcoming Northland, into a city where it seems that no one knows their neighbours anymore.

We must have looked like hobos or nutters with trekking poles. Several times we cheekily got commented on by locals, that we passed. Something like: "Yo, Mount Everest is not in New Zealand!" or "Hey it's not winter time. You can't ski here!" became a five-day routine.

Funny Aucklanders...

On top of that "climate change" in the city, we also had a long day to go. René's, Rick's and Mike's Te Araroa schedule didn't leave much room for spontaneous short days. They had to be in Bluff on the 28th of February 2016. This night, it was planned to stay at Rick's niece's place by Mt. Eden in Auckland.

Our feet were screaming out in pain from walking on concrete, as we walked towards the Auckland inlet and the ferry terminal in Devonport.

It got late and with the last kilometers walked in turbo speed, we luckily managed to jump on the last ferry into the CBD of Auckland, where we then got picked up by Sarah and her partner Clint.

Exactly one month after I had arrived in Auckland, I was back again in the city. A little bit smarter about New Zealand, a little bit lighter, physically stronger and with two or three toe nails less than I had, when I left here.

We had half a Zero Day with shopping in town when I made my promise come true: I bought a new tent. A great one. A robust one. A freestanding one. A palace. A five Billion Star Hotel.

I was happy with the sacrifice of carrying a little more weight on my shoulders, meaning I would get a better sleep in the night and hopefully a better recovery, when I purchased one of my best investments on Te Araroa Trail.

Luca left us only one day later in Ambury Park. He needed to do his own trail, he needed to be by himself. I liked our crazy Italian. He was the sort of guy with a happy-go-lucky nature, he had his own certain wisdom and peculiar views of this world. He was a dreamer. Luca had lived by himself from age 16 on, had worked in Berlin as a bartender and had then travelled and worked in Australia, where he had heard about Te Araroa Trail and had saved all his money to come to New Zealand. He was one of those hikers who didn't really seem to care about preparation or planning, he just wanted to walk. I admired his passion for walking and adventures, but sometimes doubted his capability of navigating and finding the right track. For Luca, it was too easy with our three experienced Kiwi uncles.
He never got lost, never needed to find his own way, but only follow.
It was hardly an adventure for him, so he decided to try and walk by himself. And he was right to do so.

I stretched my body in my awesome new tent in the evening. Everything seemed to have space, even my pack fitted properly in it - or as René would say "One could have a party in it." I figured jealousy was talking there as he had to crawl into his "Emergency Shelter" again that night.
I couldn't fall asleep, but instead I thought of Luca and I then began to mull over my journey on Te Araroa Trail. What was it that I expected from the trail? How did I imagine it to be, when I planned for it? Wasn't it about taking my time and doing it the way I wanted? Had I enough freedom while walking with Mike, Rick and René and the schedule?
In that moment I started to realise and it clicked. With the decision I had made in Ahipara I had accepted it to only stick with the people I loved. But I was not doing my own thing. I started to feel the chance taken from me of being free in my decisions. But I also felt the pain of having to leave awesome people that were supportive and patient and that never really forced me to walk.
I hoped for a better day of good thoughts the day after, but it didn't get better.

The Black Sheep of the Family

The next night on a campground in Auckland I met Nic, a Kiwi from Dunedin. I already knew him, not privately, but from his Give-a-Little fundraising page. He was walking the TA to raise money for his friend in Nepal whose property got destroyed in a big earthquake. While Nic was trekking in Nepal, the man had offered him a place to stay for a night, which turned into a couple of weeks. Those two weeks made them friends and Nic wanted to help him to rebuild is home.

We had a long chat, and on that occasion, he was probably not the best chat partner to make me think better about my little new issue.

Nic, as a free spirit on Te Araroa Trail, taking his time, stopping when he wanted, staying where he wanted, telling me that the hard work of saving up the money for a journey like the TA, should make it exactly that, what I wanted it to be. It hit the right spot and that night was the first night where I just couldn't fall asleep among my Kiwis.

Having spent more than a month, days and nights with them, I always got a warm comfort from having them around and now it was gone, and I wanted or needed to go. What had happened to the joy I always felt when I was with them?

The next days I spent physically walking, mulling over a plan of how to leave the group. I was okay, but I was not really happy.

In the Hunua Ranges after Auckland we met up with Luca again, who did eventually get his adventure by getting lost. He had walked in circles in the bush and eventually he ended up at the same campground that he had left in the morning, with the only difference of finding our tents pitched there now. He said: "I thought as long as I would head south" and he pointed in whatever direction, "I would eventually pop out in..." and René finished his sentence: "...In Bluff?!"

We had a good laugh about it and wondered how he could survive and actually enjoy the Northland Forests. Still it was great to see him again, and he joined us for the next day into the small town of Mercer.

Having a Zero Day scheduled we could pitch our tents for free at the local pub, Podge's Place. Everyone had a shower, we did the washing and went out for dinner. The boys chose fast food and in their defence there wasn't much else to choose from. We had had a snack at the pub already and didn't feel like too much else.

Fast Food is not really a pescatarian's first choice, but I ordered the only meat free, pescatarian option. A "fish burger" they called the spongy bread roll with tomato sauce, a bit of tartar sauce, a deep-fried fish-patty-thing and one squashy leaf of lettuce in the middle.

The prize for the worst dinner on the entire TA went to Mercer's McDonald's. Go figure! We all felt sick after.

I slept in on the Zero Day and hoped to have missed breakfast as I wanted to be alone. I was still debating what to do. So, I got up late and found trusty René and Rick waiting only for me to have breakfast.

I felt super bad. My mind still working through plans of leaving the team and me telling myself that I couldn't be happy with the way the TA was done, I just couldn't get over it. But at the same time again I couldn't get over the thought of saying goodbye to them all. They had become a real family in all this time.

But still my mind was rebelling and wanted a change. In less than a week I had become a pubescent trail teenager!

Our Zero Day went on with pizza, crackers with hummus and beer and we were lucky to have gotten to the pub on the right weekend. It was Karaoke night in Mercer and that meant that even busy Aucklanders would leave the city to have amusement and fun in that small town on State Highway 1. For shy me it was overwhelming to have so many people getting drunk in no time, singing and dancing and chatting.

Luca, me and Nic, who had arrived the night before as well, we stayed up. René, Rick and Mike went to bed, it was an early get up planned for tomorrow.

I stayed until Luca and Nic had finished their, not quite convincing but surely entertaining, Karaoke version of David Bowie's Major Tom.

One part wanting to stay up longer and experience and the other wanting to be responsible for the group, I went to bed.

Trail Journal entry for Saturday 14.11.15, Day 35

I slept in and laid in my tent for a long time in the morning. Had Pancakes for Brekkie joined by René and Rick.
We sat in the backyard of Podge's Place, the pub. Nic there, too.
Had shared pizza and a beer for lunch, out for dinner at Indian place so much better than yesterday's fish burger (yuck) and MC Sundae (yuck)

Karaoke night in Mercer's pub. Was out with Nic and Luca until 12:30am, had 1 ½ beers, the two did a Karaoke and we had chats to locals.
Really enjoyed it

I sometimes feel like on a mission and at work on the TA when we walk after the schedule. I want to have a break when I want, want to pitch the tent and finish the day when I want to.
I want to decide and not to run after appointments on a calendar.
I know I made my choice, in Ahipara, when I decided to hitch to Mangamuka Bridge and it felt right back then. But now I am not happy at all. It still would break my heart to say goodbye. I love the group and also love having them around me.
But I didn't come to New Zealand to just rattle off the trail. Yes, we make good progress kilometer and distance wise but for me it seems too fast.
I think I need a change.

In my perception, I rebelled in the morning with taking extra-long for packing up the tent, while Nic and Luca were going to have another Zero Day and a sleep in. I took extra-long for getting ready, took extra-long for breakfast and took extra-long for walking, letting me fall behind the group all time.

As I had just revealed my rebellious trail youth the day before, I had had one and a half beers in the evening, that was a lot for me, and those beers now made me pee all day. Me, who seemed to absorb her own body fluids and never stopped for a toilet break the whole time on the trail so far. I guess that was my way of being hungover from a wasted night as a trail teenager.

Literally, I was not in good spirits; the weather was as depressed as I was, and it was raining. Low clouds, a dirty Waikato River and a boring flat track on the stop banks with cow waste, or even running for life from curious young cow herds, as well as walking on State Highway 1 didn't make me feel better. I pitied myself.

At least the four of us scored a tiny little room in the Rangiriri Hotel and had a warm meal, a shower and a roof. It also meant another sleepless night for me, I couldn't fall asleep in the same room with my three friends. I moved to the lounge and couldn't sleep there either. Now most of us know what happens after two nights without proper sleep: We feel incredibly miserable. I was grumpy and stubborn, mostly at myself, I was ready to leave the group and I would carry on today come sun or rain.

It pissed down with rain and like the day before, the track was as depressing as my mood. I think that was a day were I just couldn't smile and a comment by Rick "You don't look good and not happy at all." almost made me cry. We all were soaked, and I was freezing cold, of course the strong and tough teenager that I was in the morning was gone by the afternoon.

I didn't carry on by myself, instead we got two cabins on the Huntly Campground. Rick shared a room with Mike. I shared one with René.

Even only with René in the room, I just couldn't fall asleep, lay awake and pitied my situation. I had read in the campground's guestbook about a TA girl that "got forced to walk high kilometers every day" by the group of people she was walking with. I didn't even get, that this was written in fun from her side, but it was exactly how I felt now. I did cry that night. For the fact of not being able to do my own thing, for the fact of feeling like a Grinch, as my friends deserved so much better than what I gave them at this time, and I cried about the moment of when I had to say goodbye to them. And then I fell asleep.

I heard René packing, heard René leaving the room, heard them discussing whether to wake me up or not and eventually heard them all leaving. I was awake the whole time, but I just didn't move, pretended to be asleep. I wanted them to go without me, as much as I loved them. That would have been the easiest option. I cried again.

Once they had left, I got up, and found a note with René's writing "having breakfast in town. Join us if you ready." I was not. My eyes were swollen from crying and the sleep deprivation. I just wanted to hide away but they were my Trail Family. I packed my stuff and left the room, walked to the office and Carol the camp owner offered me a lift into town to catch up with the three. She talked about how happy I must be to have these awesome and trusty friends, that would always look after me no matter what, and that it is special to have found them, that it will be hard finding anyone close like them again. I knew that, I just felt miserable and I had to stop the tears.

From the bakery were Rick, Mike and René had their breakfast we walked out of Huntly. Me in my self-inflicted misery, walking with René and chatting about me feeling useless in the group, when we passed Nathalie again. The woman I had met in Ahipara, the one I had discussed the "towel incident" with. The one I had told that I wanted to be with this group. The one that had advised me not to skip a trail part for anyone and to walk it my way. And here I was, the person that had fought for to be with the guys again, back up in Northland. The person who skipped sections for them and me the person that was now so unhappy. I acted like I was content, to not show her that she had been right. I desperately needed a Zero Day and even the boys needed one before the next section.

We crossed the Hakarimata Range towards Hamilton and for some reason, maybe because of all the chatting I had done with René, and with the weather changing as well, my mood got better that day, too. I still wanted to leave but my mind was not completely overwhelmed by these thoughts anymore.

The team had decided to take a bus for the last kilometers into Hamilton and to give us the chance of a proper rest day tomorrow. And so, we did. It must have been a hard decision from their side, too. Maybe not so much Mike, he didn't like walking on roads anyway. René and Rick tried to be purists and to walk every official kilometer of the trail. They told themselves, that one day, they would come back to walk this part again.

In Hamilton, I took the chance to do things by myself, for example beanie shopping in the morning, with the very girly question of purchasing a beanie with or without a bobble. I had issues with making decisions. How was I supposed to decide whether to leave the team or not, if I already couldn't decide between two beanies?!

I had booked a tour to Hobbiton and had a good time by myself. Got pushed through this lovely made up village, known from the Lord of the Rings and Hobbit movies, with a big tour group. While walking through the Shire I partly followed the guide's talk but got distracted by noticing many awesome tent spots as well as little streams, where I could already see myself whipping out my little water filter.

Stop it, Anna! I missed the trail already! I missed the real life and the real New Zealand with the real Kiwis!

I returned to our hostel in Hamilton, and as it is when women once leave their men by themselves at home, the three of them had been productive as well and had gotten themselves a new haircut. So, in that night I shared the room with three men that looked like bald convicts with long beards!

Onward to the forest of Pirongia the next day, I tried to have fun with my Trail Family. While Mike had hitched a fair bit, Rick and I started to become competitors in taking as many pictures of funny and creative looking letterboxes as we could along the way, to make road walking easier and entertaining. Surely, I was privileged as I owned a high zoom camera. I could comfortably stay on the other side of the road and zoom to the box, whereas Rick more or less often had to walk towards them. Good on him for doing the extra miles.

This little competition never ended in the time I was walking with him and the team.

It was a long day that took us into farmland areas, with again a curious cow herd, which was nothing new anymore by then. We now knew they didn't want to trample over our bodies and didn't want to squeeze the blood out of the dead carcasses. They were just curious and just wanted to watch us funny looking creatures.

"Oh look! Humans!"

We pitched our tents and tarps in a little forestry piece in between farmland, and by the next morning, I woke early and packed. I was on the track before everyone else. And I walked by myself. It felt great. It felt like a new won freedom and I didn't want it to be taken away, so I marched on without a break, slipping over wet grass, onto a road and then into Pirongia Forest. It indeed was the first time for me, walking without another person in the bush. And guess what, it was so easy. I knew what I had to do, I knew what I had to watch out for.

The track climbed steeply in parts through beautiful dense bush, and low clouds were hanging in the hills which made everything look spooky and enchanted. I made it to Pauhatea Hut, the first DOC backcountry hut on Te Araroa Trail, just in time before the big rain, and unpacked my wet gear, cuddled up in my sleeping bag and feasted on chocolate while watching the rain drops bursting on the windows.

I had brought enough food to stay another day, if the weather stayed rainy like that. And I swore: If my friends would carry on tomorrow in the rain, I would not. NOT. NOT.

We didn't. No one moved. The weather was bad the next day, too and no one felt like leaving the cosy and dry hut. We all had a Zero Day.

In the later hours of that day we ended up having full house, when we had Joel from Sweden, Roxelane from France, Rebecca from the States, Daniel and Josh from New Zealand, Luca, Nathalie and three Koreans popping in. All on the TA. WOW!

It was nice having many people around, we played cards, chatted, had food and naps and with the next morning we all carried on.

We followed a muddy, slippery downhill track towards a farm road, again I was reunited with Mike, René and Rick and we had a good time.

I enjoyed being with them again, after I had had yesterday to myself.

We walked across a windy airstrip and in the early evening we pitched the tents in a small bush section, had lovely dinner and a good sleep with the usual good night snoring lullaby from Mike.

Waitomo is famous for its glow worm caves and there are a lot of fun things to do. So, once we got there after a long day of walking, Luca and I booked a Blackwater Rafting Tour in one of the caves (like Canyoning but in a cave) for the next day, which would mean sleeping in for the two of us, carry on walking for my Kiwis, and also, saying goodbye to them for me!

We all had a shower with donated towels from the campground. It was always a great gesture and a moment of happiness to be offered a proper towel. Our light and small ones did not quite do the job. How happy it could make one to have a hot shower as well as a real towel. Life was so simple!

Everyone from Pauhatea Hut had arrived by the early evening. We all had a big gathering in a restaurant with pizza and beer, which was so much better than couscous and instant soup with dehydrated peas.

And with the next day came the moment I had wished for and the one that I also was scared about: It was hard saying goodbye. It already had been hard saying goodbye to my Kiwi uncles in Ahipara, but now it was even harder. There were a few tears on my side. I was never good in goodbye moments.

I watched the three carrying on, on the road out of Waitomo, and I was alone. We had spent more than 40 days together and they really had become so familiar, so normal to be with.

The team and I had talked about the Te Araroa section of the Tararua Ranges before Wellington, knowing that this was the playground of the three of them, and an important part of their TA journey, I loved the idea of joining the group for that, so rather than a proper goodbye it was more like a "See you later between Wanganui City and Palmerston North."

Still, it was heart breaking to see them go.

Got You!

The Blackwater Rafting was alright, but I didn't get half as much satisfaction out of it than I got from walking the trail. Like visiting Hobbiton, it felt too planned, fake and just unreal. Too controlled, too obvious. The best thing was the food afterwards. We got as much hot soup as Luca and I wanted with as many bread rolls as we wanted. Watch out: We were hikers and we could eat!

I woke up early the next day, it was Luca's Birthday and I invited him for a birthday breakfast in a cafe before we would hit the road.
I must have rolled my ankle during the rafting in the caves and could feel a constant pinching pain when putting pressure on my left foot while walking. As pain was nothing new, I expected it to be gone in a few days as usually those little niggles didn't last long. They came, and they went.

Luca and I got to Te Kuiti in the afternoon, where we were to be picked up by the hostel owner and in the meantime, we did our resupply for the next six days. Six days of walking and four 250gr chocolate bars, I must have bought food for eight days.
We had the most unproductive day ever, the day after. Luca as well had bought too much food and our packs were heavy. The track sign stated five hours for 15 kilometers which didn't sound encouraging either. We figured it would be tough going.
Only shortly after the sign, we found a tent site by the river with a picnic table.
I lifted my feet as the ankle was still sore and Luca had a swim. We decided to call that place our camp spot and had a lazy afternoon.
In the evening Luca made a fire and probably thought about the purpose of being, while I dearly missed René, Mike and Rick.
If I wanted to catch up with them around Palmerston North again, I had to do a fair mileage each day, knowing they would have long days on their schedule and that they would most often walk the maximum of what they could do.
I left Luca, who had a sleep in, in the morning and walked by myself, the pain in the ankle still there with every step, and the track with huge ups and downs. I ripped my backpack while sneaking over a fence, I scratched my legs, I cursed at trail markers that led from the river valley all the way up on the highest paddocks and then down to the river again and finally I

ended up on a farm road in the early afternoon. I had had enough that day, comforted myself with food at an intersection and so couldn't deal with the thought of having to walk another 27 kilometers on a road the next day. Out came the thumb. I hitched. Eventually I got picked up by a friendly Maori that I couldn't understand at all, so, I tried to talk as much as possible to avoid awkward moments of answering wrong on questions that I didn't understand right. He dropped me off at the Visitor Center of Pureora Forest where a DOC staff mentioned a group of hikers, that had come in the day before and that had left the campground this morning.

I was excited. Only one day behind the team gave me the feeling of being with them and being good in time, but keeping my new independence at the same time, as well.

I would walk to Bog Inn Hut tonight, the team accordingly must be one hut further. I partly followed the Timber Trail, a popular cycle trail in Pureora Forest, and popped up to Pureora Summit, got an awesome view, celebrated my day and carried on towards the hut. I was looking forward to having the place to myself, to having a roof and a mattress.

The stretch seemed endless, and with every minute passing without seeing the hut I swore myself to just sleep on the track tonight. The later it got, the more tired I got and all in all I must have done 30 kilometers that day plus hitchhiking the 27 kilometers on the roads.

There were voices coming from Bog Inn Hut, there was a familiar green shirt, worn by a familiar person. Mike! What the heck were they doing here?! They were supposed to be further on the track not in Bog Inn.

Rick, Nathalie, Joel, the Swedish guy, Alba, a young Spanish girl and René, everyone was there. No mattress for me that night after all. I ended up sleeping on the floor. That much about crying like a baby when we said goodbye, just three days earlier, like expecting to never to see them again. It was past 6pm and I was with the team.

Having learned my lesson and having spent three days almost by myself and with my rebellious teenage attitude, I actually was really happy to have them around again. It almost seemed like I had needed this time for myself.

What did change was my feeling for the group, I was part and I was not.

I felt freer and that I could come and leave if I wanted, I felt more independent.

The hiking days in Pureora were absolutely stunning. I walked with Nathalie for two days and we got on very well. She had done the Pacific Crest Trail in the States and she had done more tramping in New Zealand than most Kiwis will ever do. In Pureora we walked past majestic stands of 1000 year old native Rimu Trees. I remembered Rick to tell us how to recognise a female from a male Rimu: If you'd stroke their green spiky needles, the female ones would feel softer than the males, that were rougher and harder. Whenever Nathalie and I could reach a Rimu Tree I would brush their needles, and she would give the them a big hug.

Nathalie hugging a Rimu

The River

We all made it to Taumarunui with a little cheat by using a shuttle bus, that I had called at a woman's house just after leaving the forest. It was more convenient than walking on a gravel road, through farm areas, for another few hours. We were a little time pressured again as the bookings for the Whanganui River Journey needed to be done, the resupply for seven days as well as the washing of our smelly clothes, not that this would have mattered anymore; by the time we had reached Auckland weeks before, washing the smelly clothes hadn't worked anymore already. They just smelled. And we smelled after days in the bush. The cool thing is that when you stink, and you walk with smelly people it really doesn't matter. It's the smell of identification of long-distance hikers.
Our own Eau de Toilette!
Anyone that smelled like real perfume, too clean or like fabric softener? Ergo NOT a thru-hiker.
I did get creepy though - when passing people in town, I would inhale the smell of their washing powder and fabric softener and turn the head after them to get as much as possible up my nostrils. Every synthetic smell was so much more intense after not using shampoo, conditioner, deodorant, or body wash for weeks and to be fair the smell sometimes was almost too much and too fake.

We dined in a Thai Restaurant in Taumarunui and just couldn't stop ourselves buying ice cream when someone realized that the supermarket would close in less than 30 minutes. We all were hallucinating hours before, dreaming of so much food we could buy, and we didn't need to carry it, as we would be sitting on our bums in canoes for the next seven days. Fresh vegetables, tomatoes, potatoes, capsicum, fresh fruit, bananas, bread, dips, drinks, tins of vegetables, chips, chocolate, beer, one could even bring eggs. And now, none of us actually did get half the stuff they had dreamed of and wanted!
See a group of people running through the supermarket shoveling every little bit of food that they could reach in their trolleys, in the minutes that were left, until the store would shut. It almost reminded me of "Trolley Dash" a TV Show for kids and with kids that get 60 seconds in a toy store to fill their trolley with stuff that they were then allowed to keep.
"Take as much as you can get and whatever. But take it!!!"

We had our briefing by the canoe operator and had to split up into couples for our Canadian Canoes. We had Nathalie and Joel, Roxelane and Rick, I shared with René, and Mike shared a canoe with Alba. Off we were on our seven-day trip down Whanganui River from Taumarunui to Wanganui City.

The days before had been fairly dry, no heavy rain and less water in the river meant the rapids would be stronger. René and I capsized in the first rapid on the first day which was a great introduction to the river as well as made it really exciting for the next days.

Whanganui River is an official "Great Walk" (It is one of nine designated premier walking tracks in New Zealand), and the first part, from Whakahoro to Pipiriki, is the most common part, people would take. The river winds its way through farm land and into Whanganui National Park where the banks become steep and the sides of the river form a narrow gorge. It was an ancient, prehistoric feeling paddling and floating this majestic river and I felt like it was a scene cut out of the Lord of the Rings, when the Fellowship leaves Lothlorien towards Amon Hen. Hobbits ergo the girls in the front, humans ergo the boys in the back. With the sound of the movie in my head, the Fellowship of the Trail more or less stayed dry and successfully paddled day after day. Our feet had a rest and my sore ankle, I hoped, would be fine after a week without walking.

A night to remember was our stay at a Marae (Maori meeting house) further downstream. We had planned to land at the "Flying Fox Retreat" but had missed the landing. Luckily Rick talked to the senior of the local Iwi (That's the Maori tribes that own the land) and they offered us the Marae for Koha (a money based "give a little"). We all got mattresses and could take food from their pantry. While it was raining outside, we were the happiest people under the sheltering roof. Just as we had dinner, three hunters, all Maori, stepped through the door, carrying dead goats and a deer without a head into the cold store. The blood sipping out of the deer's open neck ended up on the floor and on their clothes.
The spectacle was not quite pescatarian and vegan friendly, Alba and I noticed. Bon appetit!

Whanganui River played and still plays an important role in the Maori culture. The tribes had settled in its valleys around 1100 A.D and used to cultivate the terraces as well as used the river for food supply, like the massive Whanganui eels, that apparently even creeped the famous Bear

Grylls out and made him leave the river. With the early settlers and missionaries in the 1840s the European influence arrived, and Whanganui River got famous for its riverboats, that got used for mail and resupply freights for the people that had settled along the river.

Still these days one of the main attractions during a canoe trip is stopping at the Mangapurua Landing and heading to "The Bridge to Nowhere". This is a solid concrete bridge in the middle of the bush with the sad story, of how New Zealand's government praised open fertile land to pioneer farmers, that had returned home from the First World War in Europe in 1917. After serving in the war and surviving the battles, the people then faced years of hard work and struggle against nature. They found the land too wild, rough and unsuitable for farming. One by one, the families left the area and all that remains from this time is a bridge that leads to nowhere but bush.

Still the famous steamboats officially ran on the river until the 1950s.

In 2017 Whanganui River got given its own legal identity, and it now has the rights, duties and liabilities of a legal person, and to add one more little info: One of our party was seemingly proud to be on the river journey again and especially while walking the length of his home country. Rick's ancestors used to own and run the steamboats and were part of the history of New Zealand's third longest river.

The Whanganui Journey also was an important part for me dealing with my antisocial problems. I was rather silent and quiet, watched other people chatting away about serious and not so serious stuff and began to bombard myself with negative thoughts. Why was I not chatty like the others? Why couldn't I keep conversations up? Was it because I was just not intelligent? Was it because I was hardly interested in things? Was I boring? Why and why and why. I was angry at myself and felt stink for René who had to put up with the quietest person in the team. I was always relieved once dinner and socialising was over and I could sneak off in my tent for privacy. Maybe that was also the reason for me wanting to leave the team further north. Maybe I had told myself that I would be better off without anyone else and longed for solitude.

Still I absolutely enjoyed the paddling and meeting interesting people along the way. In Whakahoro our frenchman Niko and Lucie had caught up with us, as promised, and we met Jesse, a 15-year-old boy from Palmerston North, that walked the TA in sections during his school holidays. We met American Ryan, "The Straw Hat Backpacker" who had travelled the world more than we all did together, and we shared the river with new TA faces like Andy from England and Wiep from the Netherlands and familiar faces like the group of Koreans from Pirongia.

The Whanganui River Team

René as the captain of the 'Bismarck'

By the end of the big float, René and I counted two overturns with our boat 'the Bismarck', and only got topped by the hydrophilics Rick and Roxelane, who capsized three times.

And oh, why didn't I look after my trusted friend, the backpack, sooner. Once we had arrived at the landing in Wanganui City, after two overturns and seven days on the water, I opened the supposedly dry drybag that contained my pack and out came a soaking wet, super smelly rucksack. Now it surely had its naming ceremony with the sacred waters of Whanganui River and I baptised my red backpack with the name "Stinky". Stinky took hours to dry out at the hostel that afternoon, even after he had lazily hung on the washing line, swayed in the wind and lazily baked in the sun, he smelled!
And Stinky just didn't let go of his vile smell. I had to accept that my pack, from now on, was smelling worse than my clothes for the rest of my trip.

On the Road again

I loved the trail. I loved its diversity and changing terrain, the bush and the people but if there was one thing about the TA that I didn't really enjoy on the North Island, and most of the TA hikers would probably second that, was the road walking. Not only was it hard on the feet, it sometimes was dangerous walking next to cars, smelly with their exhaust gases and incredibly loud when trucks rushed by. There is a fair amount of state highway walking on the North Island but in the defence of Te Araroa Trail, I have to say, that this trail is still just a baby. Officially opened in 2011 it has to keep up and compete with older trails out there such as the Pacific Crest Trail or the Appalachian Trail in the States. Those trails are 50 years or older and they are continuous long-distance trails, whereas the TA is still forming. There were diversions and changes to the trail when we did it and there still will be in the future.

Give it time to grow and to get established and Te Araroa will become an even better trail than it was in 2015.

From Wanganui City our next stop was Turakina Beach and that was reached by a full day of road walking on State Highway 3. YAAAY.

But bugger that! My ankle was still sore, even after seven days on the river, I could feel every single step. The, by now, familiar pain on the outside of my left foot. I didn't want to make it worse straight away and wasn't particularly keen on state highway, so I made the decision to skip this section and to get a lift with the exciting thought of maybe having a little rest day by a beach again. The first to see after so many weeks, ever since we had left Northland. "White sand, long beach, sunny warm weather and an afternoon for myself." It would be perfect.

I walked to the outskirts of Wanganui City and it was hard to get a lift.

I must have waited the longest time of all my hitchhikes so far. Cars drove past with only one person in them, leaving me thinking that there must be a green smelly cloud around me and people probably feared that this rotting odour will stick to their cars interior for many, many, many months.

Fair enough, but it wasn't just me, Stinky smelled too. It takes two to tango!

Eventually, I did score a lift with a lovely young man, who was about to visit his parents in Palmerston North and he didn't mind driving me all the way down to Turakina Beach. He was a trail angel! (trail angels are people that help out hikers on a long-distance trail. Any help, in any form, is appreciated). With his help I got to Turakina super early and had a beautiful lunch with fresh vegetables. As it was only two days to Bulls, Stinky was loaded with tomatoes and cucumbers, hummus dips, capsicum, wraps and fruit, extra heavy but extra healthy. On short stretches like that I didn't mind carrying more weight but having real food instead of snacks all the time. Yes, you can get sick of chocolates and snacks when you have it day, after day, after day. Also, believe it or not, I had gained weight, from Auckland downwards the center of the North Island, while the boys still kept on losing weight.

I figured that it must have been my chocolate consumption that was happening all the time, even though we were walking eight to 10 hours a day and surely burnt the calories off. All the sugar makes you flabby.

But, in all honesty, two days of only vegetables doesn't really make a difference.

In fact, what I learned afterwards is that we girls are likely to put on weight on a long-distance trail. Our energy distribution works different from the men's. While we bulk up muscle mass and gain weight, men are the ones that start off with more muscle mass, then build it up to a certain point and then their systems collapse and their bodies feast of muscle protein. By the time a female thru-hiker finishes a trail she looks fit and healthy, lean and muscular. A male thru-hiker in the end instead usually looks like a nearly starved to death, skinny stick figure – or like Alexander Supertramp in the movie "Into the Wild" after he had poisoned himself with the toxic plant.

We girls rule!

I pitched my tent on the little campground in Turakina and off I was to the beach. And what a beach that was. My imagination earlier was so wrong. It was dark sand and there was driftwood all the way as far as I could see. Big old tree trunks, little branches, stones, all in different colour and shapes. It was not the beach for a typical beach day. But it was great for writing things in the sand to keep a person occupied and entertained.

I created my very own Te Araroa driftwood art. With a piece of wood, I scratched TE ARAROA in the sand and filled it with little branches, roots and stones. The art looked pretty and wild and free and surely was an awesome time filler.

Mike was the second one to arrive at the campground as he had decided to hitch this section as well, it only took him longer to get a ride. Again, we girls are luckier in that perspective. Well, most of the time.

With the evening the rest of the Crew slowly fell in, they all hobbled along after having had a massive day of road walking. They had tried to get fresh water from a petrol station in Turakina settlement, but the water must have stunk like cow dung, so for the last hour or more they hadn't had any liquids, except for maybe a coffee, and it was steamy hot on that day.

Niko, Lucie, René, Mike, Rick and I carried on the next day, only a day walk to Bulls where René's and Mike's Brother Robert would pick us up and take us to his place in Feilding. In the early morning, except for heading to Turakina Beach, which would have been the right choice, we made our way through a little pine forest and, like Hansel and Gretel, got lost in the woods, bashed through stands of pine trees, broke branches off to get through the forest and brushed through the scrubs back towards the beach. We scrambled down the dunes and ended up where we should have been already, back on the official trail.

The beach was a little reminder of 90 Mile Beach and Northland even though it still was black sand and a lot of driftwood, which was great for entertainment as it came in different shapes and sometimes it was animal shapes and sometimes it looked like figures from old tales.

From the beach we entered another pine forest and got onto a backcountry road, we walked in the heat of the day. I walked ahead and while turning around, to look for the Crew, there were five glimmering figures walking in the distance.

Came Bulls, Rick and I competed in our letterbox game, took pictures of as many fancy letterboxes as we could and with an ice cream and coffee in town, we waited for Robert to bring us home to his place, a lifestyle block by Feilding.

A lifestyle block is a property for people that want to experience farm life. They keep a few sheep, some keep chickens, bees or other animals. Most of the people are after living an alternative sustainable and self-sufficient life rather than a residential city or town life, but most of them keep working in their most often super busy and well-paid jobs, to keep their lifestyle block maintained. What sounds lovely is a lot of work and this lifestyle they are looking for is often not achieved.

The old villa on Robert's property was beautiful, the ceilings were high and the rooms large, filled with quirky old furniture that made up for a cool atmosphere. I got my own room, or as René would say "Prinzessinnen Zimmer", "princess room" upstairs and had a lovely shower with shower gel and shampoo. On top of that, we had a nice dinner together with Robert, his partner Maree and her son Cam.

Palmerston North was a day hike away and again would take us along State Highway 3 through meaningful places with funny names like 'Bunnythorpe'. But there was no Bunnythorpe for Mike and me, we lazily bused to Palmy where we met up with René and Rick in the afternoon as they, of course, had walked that part. Naughty us!

After shopping in Auckland and Hamilton, Palmerston North was another attractive address for outdoor gear shopping. I went off looking for new quick drying shorts, while the three caught up with Mike's and René's nephew Michael Junior and Rick's nephew Ben in the Robert Harris Cafe in the center of Palmerston.
I joined them later and proudly showed my new purchased shorts. René loved the idea, left us, came back and he had gotten himself new shorts as well. The same ones as mine, but the boys' version. Copy cat!

It turned out that the owners of the Robert Harris Cafe, Barney and Rose, were the parents of Jesse, the young boy we had met on Whanganui River. Barney and Rose are real trail angels. While they were supportive of their son's dream to complete the TA before finishing school (Which he achieved!), they also supported other hikers and we were about to be spoiled with a big breakfast the next morning, only for a little Koha from each of us.

Mountains to City

The Tararua Ranges section was one of the things I was curious about at home already, while planning for my TA adventure. For all of the TA I had counted 20-25 kilometers a day of hiking to make it to Bluff in a good time. While I planned, like the non-experts do, with my laptop at home, on my lap, in bed, I had my Google Earth Globe up and yellow and red "daily distance" needles would poke out from the GPX track that I had downloaded. So, also for the Tararuas my average mileage was the same as for every other stretch of the TA, roughly 25km per day.

Little we know when we sit there in our cosy rooms without any idea of how it really could be. Just because the map is flat doesn't mean the track is also flat.

After having our breakfast at Barney's and Rose's cafe in Palmerston North, Niko, Lucie, René, Rick, Mike and I headed on the road, it was another full day of road walking. We passed the agricultural sides of Massey University as we were leaving the city behind. Windy roads led us along green hills, farmland and private properties, we had lunch by a little stream followed by another long walk on tarseal.

It also was another day of continuing the letterbox competition with Rick. That game just never got boring.

Winding its way along a river, a gravel road led us out of cellphone coverage and into Kahuterawa Reserve. We passed a carpark with pine trees, a picnic table and a toilet. A great camp spot and everything was perfect for the night, except for the water in the river, which was brown and not very inviting. But, if you don't have a choice, you take what you can get. The pine trees gave us shelter, as it was supposed to rain in the night and morning, and the picnic table was great for a change to not having to eat on the ground. That evening we dined like civilised people do.

And it started to rain in the morning. With my tent I had the option of packing it without getting the inside wet. I had never tried it before, but knowing I had to sleep in it another night, I tried and failed. It took me ages to handle the procedure and in the end it all ended up wet. I guess it is always worth the try. I never tried it again.

The foothills of the Tararua Ranges welcomed us with low clouds and drizzle as we walked on a forestry road beneath cut down pine trees, remains and stumps still visible as well as some left-over logs. It made the whole scenery look spooky and unforgettable.

That evening we ended up at a water reservoir, one of the three man-made Mangahao Dams, that supply water to a power station and to the Horowhenua region and towns like Shannon and Levin. It was an unsettling area, it was wet and windy, the concrete walls of the dam made the place look dark and unwelcoming, as well as the fact, that the road was used by four-wheel drivers and obviously had seen quite a few rowdies during all the years. Finding a tent site was hard, with the wind blowing from every direction and almost no bush to shelter away from, but eventually Rick found a little narrow track with prickly gorse bushes, that sort of sheltered us a little bit from the wind, and we declared it to be the best place possible.

As I said, it "almost" sheltered us. When the tents were halfway up, a gusty wind nearly blew my house into the gorse but with his bush craft skills, Rick fixed it to the ground using large rocks, and with the help from Niko, who let one of the rocks slip, my tent ended up with two patches of duct tape that evening, too.

It is a weird thing to think of being surrounded by million liters of water in those lakes but it being inaccessible for thirsty hikers. It was a dry night in drinking water perspective but with the wind howling and René getting up in the night to fix a puddle of water in his "Emergency Shelter" and me secretly comfortably hugging my dry sleeping bag, knowing that this wouldn't happen to me, still a successful finish.

From gravel to proper bush track the next morning the Tararuas showed the sheer beauty of plants and trees, beautiful little streams running by, and as it was still New Zealand and still Te Araroa Trail, it was mud intensive, too. Mud comes in all varieties!

In New Zealand's bush one can encounter very squishy, moist, splashing mud. Very thick, squelchy mud. Mud that is dark brown. Fawn mud. Almost orange looking mud. Mud that had gotten dissolved in water puddles. Mud, that looks like firm ground but actually isn't. Deep mudholes. Shallow mud puddles. Loamy mud, clayey mud, silty mud, sandy mud, quick drying, super slippery mud and sometimes mud is even there, where you wouldn't expect mud. No matter what kind of mud it was, it was always the most rewarding process to scrape it off the legs, arms and face once I had a shower when out in civilisation.

Having now spent more than two months walking the trail here in New Zealand, a muddy patch that was ankle deep had become a joke, it became a little puddle compared to mid-thigh deep mud holes that seemed to swallow your leg and that wanted to make your shoes their own by ripping them off your feet, if not just the shoes, sometimes it felt like the mud wanted to rip off your leg as well.

Be aware of those little sneaky mud monsters, they are hungry for hikers. At that point most of them hardly ever saw 20 people a month. Fair enough. I'd be starving too. Still, lucky mud monsters, with the increasing popularity of the TA, the years of starvation hopefully are over.

This day we met a few day hikers though, and it was a pleasant walk, crowned by a pick-up service from Rick's sister Deb, her husband Paul and her family. We got a bed, a shower and proper dinner that didn't include instant Cup a Soup and it's still not very creative and more and more unappealing friend "Couscous".

It was an awesome arrangement by Rick and it really paid off knowing my Kiwis. I had the chance to meet other local families, and I guess my trail surely would have been emptier without those experiences and connections.

Deb's boys, Ben and Jake, dropped us off in Levin for our resupply. The hills were waiting and with them the first real serious tramp. With four days' worth of food and heavy bellies, as supermarkets were still paradise for hikers that had the hiker hunger turned on, we got driven towards our next section, towards the hills, covered in dark clouds, hanging over the tops as if they were saying "Come to us and you will be swallowed and gone forever."

With René, Mike and Rick being Tararua boys, they were home, and they knew the tracks as well as the huts. It must have been a fascinating feeling to actually walk home, they now were so close to Wellington, after almost 1600kms. Already back in Germany the imagination of a "walking home" trip left me with a feeling of achievement and pride. So, I guess it was the same for them now.

With their knowledge of the ranges, the three, Lucie and I went on a sightseeing detour, whereas Niko had decided to stick to the official TA Route. Sorry Niko, but you missed out. The Kiwis led us European girls towards Ohau River Route. Meaning free walking without any trail markers and again "pick your own route."

The cold crystal-clear running water of Ohau River was heaven for my still sore ankle. It had become stiff and the pinching pain was a permanent follower with every step, which made it challenging to walk in a river bed at the same time.

Like little ducklings we first waddled after Mike and Rick, crossed the river in the places where they had crossed and slowly got more confident as we walked towards the gorge, they had told us about. We had fallen trees to balance over, waist deep crossings as well as slippery rock climbs.

In the middle of the river we then encountered the "touch-me-and-I-make-you-slip-and-bang-your-head-against-another-rock-and-make-you-drown-and-die"-rock, that forced me and Rick on all fours, whereas René with the imaginary sounds of the Lord of the Rings and the grace of Legolas the Elf, balanced over it. Show off – again!

Come hut come excitement, come slip and fall. I managed to stay as dry as possible until I spotted South Ohau Hut. With a slip-sliding-stumble over the rocks I ended up in the water just before reaching it and eventually got there with a wet bum.

South Ohau, lies beautifully nestled in between the forks of two streams, surrounded by native bush, Rimu Trees and Ponga Ferns. I could already see myself spending weekends in this awesome place; tucked away from civilisation with a private river, and the hut deck offered stunning views. But no rest for the wicked, we gobbled our lunch, signed in the hut book and then we were off to Te Matawai Hut.

Just before leaving we got a little information from Mike "It's a very steep hill, if you start climbing too fast your calves will not forgive you!" and a note from René "Once you're up at the twin trees it's pretty much flat all the way to Te Matawai."

It was a hell of a climb. A calf killer. This was, what I learned afterwards: "Just a normal Tararua climb." With no mercy on our legs the track lifted itself up, in an almost straight line, from the river level. Hands had to be used to hold on to roots, and the poor calf muscles were pumping and screaming for blood for 30 minutes. No mercy from Mike's and Rick's side either "No sitting down. No stopping. Keep climbing."

The twin trees were close. Two big trees on either side of the track marked the beginning of the apparently "pretty much flat" part. Just kidding, for legs that just climbed hundreds of meters of altitude, every little up and down was easily misinterpreted as a huge drop and climb.

I chose René to walk with, as I considered him the gentler and non-forcing one of the three, who probably would let me have a rest every now and then. So, we did and ended up being the last ones to arrive at Te Matawai Hut at 900 meters altitude, found Niko, Alba and Joel as well as Jonny and Rebecca, the English couple from Northland, and the delight of a fire that was still a baby but about to grow to heat us all and to hopefully sort of dry our clothes and wet socks.

We found ourselves in a low cloud the next morning, the fire in the evening didn't dry our stuff and we had to put on wet socks and wet boots before we started our big day. I think from all days on the TA, that day was the longest in hours with the shortest of kilometers. It was a ridge line walk above the bush line of absolute world class. With the low cloud there was no visibility on the tops except for the few meters of track ahead of you, beside you, and the colourful packs of the hikers, who seemed like little ants, slowly walking in a line, following their leader ant Mike to their destination. It was a harsh, unforgiving environment and pretty at the same time. The Tararuas now showed their real face to me and my thoughts were going back to my days of planning, sitting in my room and counting 25 kilometers a day. I think we did eight kilometers in maybe six to eight hours and what had looked like a forest on Google Earth turned out to be bold, exposed ridge lines. Rugged, muddy and slippery tracks led us over small and big peaks with really cute names like Pukematawai and Puketoro, that were anything but lovely - there was no sidling around, it was straight ups and downs with little rock climbing actions involved. I was buggered when I reached Dracophyllum Hut, a small two-person shelter painted in bright orange. Adding to my stiff and aching left ankle my knees terrorised me through and through. I felt like I couldn't carry on anymore. I quietly, in desperation, decided that this would be it. I would stop at Dracophyllum and leave the group. I was physically not capable to walk anymore, had to hold back tears of grief about it all and told the team about my plans.

A "No!" from René and a "No, No, No, No!" from Rick sealed the pact of taking my first ever pain killers on the trail. I am not a fan of drugs. Pain is a sign from my body telling me I do damage and that I needed to stop and rest. Never was any pain or ache a reason for me to take pills. I had been stubborn and reluctant. But now it was the time and I swallowed two pills after lunch. As I was not experienced in the field of painkillers, I was waiting for the pain relief to kick in every minute and I was waiting for my stomach to cramp and actually to get super sick after taking the drugs. None of the last happened but the pain in the knees did become bearable and with good old Rick, who had troubles with his knees as well, I did spend an amazing time, just the two of us walking together. He gave me the confidence to carry on walking slowly but steadily and told me we would reach Nichols Hut before the bad weather would kick in. Our last out-in-the-open stretch after a little piece of sheltered forest was signaled by René's voice from maybe 100 meters below us. Still in the clouds and mist, we couldn't see Nichols Hut, but it surely was there right in time.

To our surprise we found Lucie without Niko but with food and a written message. "I carried on, give my Baby a cooker to cook a dinner, see you tomorrow in Waitewaewae Hut. Love, Niko."

I did like Niko and he obviously had been in a walking rage and just didn't want to stop - but boy, you don't do that to your girlfriend. Lucie was seemingly unimpressed by that move.

That evening we got the wood burner cranking and with another couple of painkillers as dessert I fell asleep.

What we didn't get to see while staying at Nichol's was the apparently stunning view from the long drop toilet. Shame about that.

The weather didn't improve over night and with our Kiwis that had planned on a really short day down the ridge to Waitewaewae Hut we gladly got to lie in, had breakfast and pain killers in bed, as well as a few naps to wait out the worst of the weather. Our timing was great and by the time we were packed, the heavy winds were gone, and we climbed over Mount Crawford towards the track junction and Shoulder Knob and began descending from the tops back down into the bush.

We had gotten the taste of how hard it is, climbing up to the tops, a few days before and Te Araroa-like it made you level your altitude meters, by dropping steeply, back down to river level.

Only two hours to Waitewaewae Hut the sign had said on the ridge. "Surely that wouldn't be hard" but with buggered knees and ankle from the days before this descend stayed in my head. Going steeply downhill for two hours means your knees hardly bend in that time, but if they sometimes do, then it will feel like the joint capsule gets a massive stretch in an unknown bend position and it is bloody painful. Another set of pain killers didn't really help, but at least the brain was satisfied with sort of a placebo effect.

The nature around the track was a blur; I guess I only lived for the moment of seeing the next hut.

Only just before reaching the river, the track levelled out again, and we crossed a long swing bridge with only another 15 minutes to Waitewaewae Hut, a great hut in an awesome setting, again. Everyone took off their smelly clothes, got changed into dry gear and I was ready for painkillers with my second lunch.

Again, we had a fire going, Jonny and Rebecca arrived in the evening and we all prepared dinner. What happened now was just another act of Anna-stupidity and added to more content in the "That was dumb" book.

I was still using my Methylated Spirits stove and accidentally left some of the fluid in the little container from the night before. As I was a little bit reluctant to give my pot a good wash (call me yucky, but a dirty bowl was just fine with me) some of the spirits had leaked into my pot and had ended up in my dinner.

There was a strange bitter taste to my usually super delightful cup a soup mushroom couscous that night and I went to bed feeling a little funny.

I felt like shit the next morning, I felt like I had been eating raw onions and garlic, which now made my face swell up during the night, or maybe like after Mum's French onion soup, that I loved to eat but surely only on a weekend, knowing about the antisocial results, the day after. I could only open my eyes to little slits and my cheeks were puffed.

Teasing comments like "Come on, Anna, open your eyes. Come on, wake up, open them." or my friends asking me whether I had partied to hard, made everyone laugh and for René's daily people selfie I tried to give a big grin. That didn't really work and I realised that I had partly poisoned myself with Meths in my pot.

The meths-morning-face!

Plenty of water and a good day's walk made my body flush out the toxins, and my face look normal again. What a transformation!

We followed the track down towards Otaki Forks, another popular recreational area and one of the main entrances in the Tararua Ranges. Niko, Lucie, Alba and Joel stayed in Parawai Lodge close by and we four, the Kiwis and I, were supposed to be picked up again. Phil, a friend of René's lived in Otaki and had offered to put us up for a night or two. We waited in the shelter by the car park but there was no Phil, in fact there were no cars at all.

Otaki Forks has like lots of DOC areas its own park ranger and our own personal Mr. DOC, René, tried to get hold of him and came back with the news. They had had a massive landslip on the road just the day before we arrived, it was impassable for cars and also crossing on foot was not recommended. No wonder Phil wasn't there.

The park ranger offered us all a lift on his quadbike and gave us the "okay" for carefully crossing the slip. The ride was exciting. Mike and I lifted the packs on the front of the quad, sat behind the ranger and got thrown around while he raced around the corners on this windy gravel road and its big potholes that were spread out all over it. We were accompanied by his dog that was thrilled to run as close to the bike as he could.

I was so grateful for the little lift. I literally was in one pain. Knees and ankle both were sore, I was smelly and felt yuck.

Past the slip we walked with Jonny and Rebecca and got cellphone coverage after quite a while of hammering our feet on tarseal. The poor feet were not used to that one anymore, and the road walking business after a few days of soft tracks in the bush, always got them by surprise.

The moment of relief came with Phil and his car and the lift that took us into Otaki, where we got dropped off at his house, a flash place with a big lounge. Josie his wife had already prepared dinner for us.

After a shower and clean up we had plenty of salads, breads as well as meat for the carnivores. We had dessert and after that lollies.

I had dreamed about real food the hours before and had imagined the big portion I would eat, but in this very moment I only managed one plate for dinner.

Supposedly tummies shrink with the portions we eat, as we hikers spent more time eating from our tiny but obviously well sized pots and bowls our tummies had adapted to the tinier portions but wanted more frequent input. Nowadays with food portions that burst the size of the plate, or with the increasing popularity of XXL restaurants, we just don't realise our changing eating habits anymore and that it really is not normal to feast like that.

I decided that my ankle was too sore to carry on the next day and texted my friend Verena, who works as a Massage Therapist in Waikanae, the next township south of Otaki. I had sent a little gear parcel to her place when I got sorted in Auckland, back in October.

The boys got a lift back to the landslip before Otaki Forks, to then continue walking on the trail and Verena's boss Debbie was going to pick me up in the afternoon.

I had plenty of time at Phil's and Josie's and I was hungry. I had fresh bread and cereals for breakfast, I had another shower, and I was naughty and sneaked a fair amount of lollies from the box in the kitchen, and another few.

I met Debbie at the supermarket and she drove me into Waikanae. Turned out that her house and work was just two kilometers off the trail, in the little settlement of Reikorangi. I wondered whether Alba or Joel needed a place to stay for the night, so Debbie and I had a little run around in the car, to try and find them on the roads. We didn't but we met René, Mike and Rick. I got a hug from René like we hadn't seen each other for four weeks, and while Rick and René decided to walk into Waikanae – remember - they were purists, Mike gladly accepted a lift into town.

Dinner with Verena and the Hartley Family was lovely, the whole family was there; Wayne, Debbie and the daughters Jess, Laura and Elysia as well as Alex, their son. It was December, summer school holidays and Uni was finished as well.

I got to meet the family's pets Luna, the Chinchilla and Bear, a big, a seriously big, but friendly dog, and as I already had two showers at Phil's, I happily declined the offer for another one.

We sat in the lounge, chatted, had a drink and Debbie gave me a wonderful foot massage for my sore ankle. She didn't even mind the fact that I had lost several toe nails due to constant pressure from wearing my boots.

I received my little gear parcel and found that after all, I didn't need anything from it. There were spare little plastic bottles that I had thought I might use for oil or salt, there were all sorts of things and funnily enough a pair of razors. Silly girl. I only grabbed new duct tape and first aid stuff as I found these to be the only reasonable things to carry around with me. Okay, and one of the razors!

Verena taped my ankle the next morning, we got in her car to get to Waikanae where I met up with René and Rick, said my goodbyes to Verena and off we hikers were, down the Waikanae River Walkway towards the beach and the Kapiti Coast townships Paraparaumu and Paekakariki with the destination Pukerua Bay.

Halfway down the beach we met up with friends of René's, who some had walked the TA back in 2012. They were great to talk to, especially as most of them were DOC people and they had been through the whole trail journey by themselves. Together we treated ourselves to lunch in a cafe in Paraparaumu which got us going until Paekakariki and the next cafe.

We really lived the dream. I guess if it wasn't for the Kiwis, I wouldn't have stopped in restaurants and cafes, but mostly supermarkets and little stores, which would have been cheaper but definitely not as yummy as a warm vegetarian pie with a salad.

The group of Emma, Nik, Kirsten and Gen had parked their car in Paekakariki and with the German invalid hiker, aka me, the five of us cruised along State Highway 1 towards Pukerua Bay and again to a colleague of René's for the night. Karen, from South Africa, and her husband owned this beautiful place, overlooking the Kapiti Coast and Kapiti Island. Lucky people they were. And to my surprise they had cats! Even luckier people they were now!

As I was first to arrive with the drop off service, I had a shower and chilled on the couch, while waiting for the rest of the Crew to arrive. Again, we had a beautiful dinner with homemade bread, salads and another morbid gain for me: the second foot massage of the day. The first one from Rick on the beach before Paekakariki and now a massage from Mike.

As I said: Living the Dream!

The life of a thru-hiker is pretty simple: You eat! You walk! You sleep, and you repeat!

In Pukerua Bay we ate, and we slept, and after breakfast in the morning, we walked. It was planned to reach the North Island TA terminus in Wellington in three days and also to slow down the speed once we would reach New Zealand's capital.

I got my "little panic attack of the day" in a supermarket in Porirua, where I did my resupply. At the counter I just couldn't find my overseas credit card anymore. I had purchased a little snack a few hours before in a cafe and had accidentally left it behind. Now that's a very unreasonable thing to do and again entered the "that was dumb" rubric. I was in a mental shock.

What if someone just took it?

What if I never got it back?

What if this was the end of my TA journey?

What if I had to starve to death, now that I didn't have any money left?

"What if you just ring up the cafe and ask them first before you start panicking?" Rick asked. Fair enough! Sigh…., old people, they always know the answers to things in life…

Said and done, I explained to the lady on the phone what had happened and where I was. I gave her René's address in Wellington and also told her I'd be there for a few days, as we had Christmas ahead, for René, Mike and Rick family time, and therefore a few Zero Days. The answer "Yes, we found the card, and no worries, we post your credit card to you." was honestly a big relief.

Although I was a destitute TA hiker, and broke in terms of money for the next days, I was wealthy and rich with friends surrounding and supporting me, giving me the feeling that everything would be alright.

To decrease the amount of road walking but also the hilly Wellington region was probably inviting Te Araroa Trail planners to send hikers up a big hill, just to make them descend into a valley again shortly after. I could see the planners sitting around the table with a little naughty grin on their face and tenting their fingers a la Mr. Burns from The Simpsons, while defining the Up-Down-Up-Down-Route. "Excellent."

Funnily enough, and proof that New Zealand is just a 'little village', where everyone knows everyone, we climbed up the hill by Camp Elsdon, in Porirua, on a gravel road and had two young guys passing us. One of them I recognised from my flights to Auckland. It was Lars! What a surprise. We both were excited and had a little catch up on our own individual journeys through Middle Earth. How cool to happen, to be at the same time at the same place from all the places in New Zealand one could be. And as I said in the beginning, our journeys had been really different.

I caught up to the Crew and we entered Spicers Forest, a little pine tree colony just before Ohariu Valley. Camping was not permitted, but as one of the team noticed by looking at the sign, our tents didn't look half as similar to the one shown on the little picture, we therefore agreed to just go for it and find the next suitable flat, and hopefully hidden place, to set up camp for the night. We picked a really cosy one, behind a few bushes off the track, by a little stream.

Sadly, with having the pine trees around, and their needles on the ground, they make the soil too acid for most of the native plants to grow and the water in the stream was not quite as clear as the streams in the Tararua Ranges. René really hates those trees. He explained to us that it is only possible to grow three generations of pine trees on the same ground before it loses all nutrients to grow other plants. New Zealand's land and grounds sadly get raped every year, thousands of acres of land. They cut down native bush to farm and they cut down native bush for forestry. Most of the logging forests are internationally owned, for example by Chinese investors or American ones. The logged trees then get exported overseas for making furniture, which then get sold back to New Zealand and other countries. Also, pines are introduced to New Zealand and their seeds resistant to almost every condition. DOC is permanently battling wilding pines in their National Parks. Shame about it, for us Europeans, the warm sweet smell of a pine forest is probably the loveliest memory of summer holidays by the sea.

René's daughter Vanessa joined us the next day from Ohariu Valley into the CBD of Wellington. She was as bubbly as her dad, "a female René version" she would call it, and Ness was super easy to connect and talk to. Even though I was a stranger to her, she didn't seem to mind and really made it comfortable to walk with. She made us laugh as she carried immense amounts of water and a week's supply of chocolates, but after climbing up Mount Kaukau in the heat, our water supply went alarmingly short, and we all were grateful for Ness having so many bottles spare.
I guess everyone did benefit from that. We didn't die of thirst and dehydration and Ness's backpack got super light.
The other benefit of walking with locals was to be invited at another friend's place, just one of the first streets in, after we had entered Wellington. Jon, again a friend of René's and Ness's, and his Mum had made homemade scones with jam. Enough for all. Yum.
Jon had this funny tweak with German books or so, that he tried to explain to me. I had no idea what he was talking about but acted as professional as a German can.
Wellington, "the coolest little capital in the world" was one interesting place of a city; knowing to have civilisation around you, there were still natural corners hidden away from all, making you feel like being in the bush again, except for all the lovely smelling and clean looking, strolling people that must have turned their noses away, when a group of smelly hikers passed their way in Ngaio Gorge.
Ngaio Gorge was the place were René and his older brothers, Mike and Robert, grew up playing in and surely, they had had their small and big adventures when balancing over trees, building dams in the stream and discovering, for the public closed, tunnels. They scraped their knees, got bruised and probably once or twice nearly killed themselves while playing. Aaaaah yes, a childhood in the 60's and 70's was so much different to ours. We had Lara Croft in Tomb Raider, scraping her legs, getting injured and getting killed by aggressive animals, dinosaurs or humans.

The team had an early takeaway dinner in Wadestown, a part of Wellington that has these beautiful old Victorian style designed houses. Now, in summer time, they looked cute with colourful flowers in the gardens and especially in combination with the lovely blue sky. Wadestown also has a super steep road going up to Tinakori Hill which made Ness and me wish we'd never had eaten these big portions of fatty chips beforehand.

We dragged our lazy bodies and packs up the hill and AGAIN to our surprise the sign telling us "camping prohibited" showed a picture of a tent we just could NOT relate to. Our tents just didn't look like that!

Rick and René knew a place off the tracks, on Tinakori Hill, to pitch the tents and to finish our day. What a camping spot it was; we were high above the city overlooking the CBD, the Rugby Stadium, and Wellington Harbour, and it got even more impressive by night with all the city lights around us.

I shared my tent with Ness, we had all the chocolates she had carried for dessert, and we were a good match while sleeping: No condensation issues the next morning when we packed up again.

We had a cafe breakfast in town with Maja, a Croatian Canadian woman, who had met René on the Camino de Santiago in 2013, and who has an accent I could barely understand. She was now a PHD student at Victoria University and lived at René's place. I handed my smelly Stinky to her and her boyfriend and made the hard decision again, to not carry on, but seeing a physiotherapist for my ankle, instead. I was super disappointed to again miss out on a section of the TA, and especially with it being the last section of the North Island.

Ness was loyal and waited with me. Like an old couple we sat on a bench at "The Beehive", the building where New Zealand's government sits and thanks to her bubbly nature, she managed to stop my grief and the tears. The physio herself was this super tiny, lean, older woman, but boy, she pulled and twisted my ankle around, in all directions that were possible.

I thought back to my time as a physio student and our manual therapy teacher. He would have been impressed with that show. The little bones in my foot got thrown around, it cracked and ground. She stretched my legs and I almost was in tears again, not for the grief of missing out on the walk, but for the feeling of being ripped into pieces by that tiny woman with strong arms and hands.

It worked. She freed my ankle and I was walking without pain for an entire day.

This experience made Ness and me hungry.

"What's for lunch, Ness?"

"What do you feel like? I can show you some places."

Where there was Vanessa, there always was food. No starving! She was like a TA hiker. I loved her!

We had Kebabs in town, she showed me around Wellington, and in the afternoon, we caught a bus to René's house in Houghton Bay, caught up with the group and walked the last piece of the North Island as a team with Niko and Lucie, René, Mike, Zorro the dog, Rick, Kirsten, René's work colleague, who had already joined us on the Kapiti Coast, and Wiep our Dutchie from Whanganui River.

Ness baptised Rick due to his fluffy, white-gingery beard with a traditional Santa Hat from a $1 Store, and from that day on he had his nickname "Santa". He was the first one of the team to get a trail name.

It is a long-distance trail tradition in the States, for people to give each other new names and with them new identities. People would be called after, for example, a certain food they were always eating, a special characteristic like their look, or after a misadventure that someone had heroically survived, or really anything that made it easy for others to identify them.

With our Santa we walked along the south coast of Wellington towards the little TA terminus stone on a playground in Island Bay. We had finished the first 1600km of about 3000km.

The TA stone in Island Bay

It was Christmas and family time for the Kiwis. We all said goodbye to Mike and Rick, who got picked up to have their well-earned rest from the trail. We "kids" played for a little while longer on the playground to celebrate our adventure.

My twin Julia had come to New Zealand for a holiday, had already spent a few days in the country, and we picked her up from the train station to have her around for Christmas time at René's.
Also, our Italian Luca had skipped sections to spend Christmas with us and also to be ready for the South Island leg of the TA.

Shame about my ankle, which blew up just on the 25th, and even with painkillers it was terribly sore. The positive news was the arrival of my credit card with a personal note from the cafe people that said "Hope this arrives okay. Have a great New Zealand summer tramping!"

It was a little different Christmas from what Julia and I used to have at home. And even though I was never a big fan of it, I have to admit that celebrating it in summer with 30 degrees with a BBQ is positively odd, especially when all the music you hear is "Dreaming of a white Christmas" and the stores are decorated with Santa Clauses that wear their heavy as coats, boots and hats. Surely, they would sweat in the heat of summer. How about inventing a Kiwi-Santa in shorts or togs (Kiwi word for swim suit) with sunglasses and Jandals?

All in all, I spent three days in Wellington mostly with Ness and Julia, and we had a good time in Houghton Bay. Nevertheless, three days was long enough. I was ready to go back to my simple life without the christmassy overload of things and food and stressed people.

"Change is good" They say

Julia and I took a plane to Blenheim. Rick, Mike and Luca the ferry to Picton, and René and his partner flew into Picton to walk Queen Charlotte Track together, their "Glamping" trip or "glamour camping". Small packs, beds to sleep in, prepared meals and showers. It surely was lovely and nice but in all honesty: I actually enjoyed carrying my heavy smelly Stinky, sleeping in the tent, cooking my usual trail meals and not having a shower, as well as being among the group. Next to the glampers we thru-hikers looked so much more adventurous and wonderfully filthy. In René's defence, he didn't look much different to us either with his big, almost matted looking beard.

We twins made it to Picton with a few lifts from strangers. We booked the boat shuttle to the trail head of Queen Charlotte Track, had a resupply and Fish 'n' Chips in town. We saw three women who looked like TA hikers and we saw a couple that had trekking poles and proper backpacks, too. I was excited. Like starting a new chapter of a book, this was the start of a new chapter on the TA.

The South Island welcomed us with different views, new plants and also new birds. A sneaky brown hen like bird, aka the Weka, a curious little bugger, that is keen on anything that looks like food. They knew exactly where people stopped for lunches and breaks and hung out in those places, or they would suddenly run out of the bush and across the tracks chasing each other. They were fun, but you had to be cautious about them and really protect your holy, precious food. An American girl walked into a campground on Queen Charlotte Track, super excited about her being so lucky to have seen three Kiwi Birds today. We sadly had to tell her that this was most likely not the case and that she had seen the Wekas doing their Weka-thing. Admittedly though, those birds may have a little similarity with Kiwi Birds. But really only little.

Luca caught up to the group. He and my sister got along quite well, and they had a lot to chat about. Both loved playing the guitar and both had learned it by themselves without a proper teacher. I made new contacts with the couple and the three women, we had seen in Picton, just before going on the shuttle boat.

Maud and Guillaume from France. Those two just seemed so familiar from the first moment on and whenever we talked about them, there was never a doubt: There is no Maud without a Guillaume. They just have the right "Zing". Maud for me was, like Alba, Lucie and Nathalie an important female hiker and surprisingly comfortable to be with.

The three women Marlies, Sandie and Sarah were doing the South Island Te Araroa, they must have been the female version of Rick, René and Mike. They later would look after me like aunties would.

Queen Charlotte Track was easy to walk, it was a hiking-highway. We thru-hikers had become walking-machines and we could walk faster and longer than anyone else and everything seemed so easy for us now. We had grown up on the North Island, found our thru-hiking feet, and now we were TA adults. We knew what we had to do and how to do, everything was automatic. Packing the backpacks, setting up the tents in the evening and taking them down in the morning. What had taken me 40 minutes to an hour, back on 90 Mile Beach, now took me less than 15 or 20 minutes. We all had found our individual rhythms during the day and knew each other like family. Faces of strangers had become normal, the verbal and nonverbal language between us had improved and we just worked very, very well as a team.

Queen Charlotte Track was also very scenic. I remember Julia commenting on one of the views, while looking at pine forests and the sounds "It almost looks like the Black Forest." Indeed, New Zealand has so many facets and it always happens that you climb a mountain and the view would remind you of the European Alps or parts of France or anywhere else, and I bet Americans or Canadians, who travel to New Zealand would probably say exactly the same. Maybe this is one of the reasons that New Zealand, for so many tourists, feels so familiar and almost a bit like home when they come here for travelling.

René joined us on the last day out to Anakiwa. I had missed him as a chat partner and was happy to have him back. Over the North Island his beard had grown so big that his cheeks looked puffy and the slightly ginger, brown colour of the beard with a few white hairs in between just called out for the trail name "Chipmunk". His suggestion "Bergmann", "Mountain Man" got declined straight away. Rick didn't have a choice either! And who wouldn't want to have such a cute trail name like "Chipmunk" anyway?

René was considerate with me and my sore ankle, so we were the last ones to race into Anakiwa to catch the little kiosk before it shut the blinds. Naughty food tastes so much better when you know that you deserve it after a long walk. The ankle gave me grief and Rick organised a lift with a travelling family to the Linkwater Campground. I was happy and then I was angry (not really) as on the way we passed all these amazing letterboxes, which I knew Rick would pass on foot to take pictures of them. Maybe he had known about them already and did it on purpose to cut me out of the competition and to call himself the winner!? I sensed a conspiracy and felt a little betrayed.

In the hurry of leaving the family's car on arrival at the campground I forgot to take my trekking poles with me. The car drove off and I had Stinky. I only had Stinky. My poles were gone.

But then, the trail provided again. The family returned, one of the kids had found the poles under the seats. That was like Christmas and Birthday together. I was grateful for those trail angels, and I begged my poles for pardon for just forgetting them in a stranger's car.

At Linkwater Campground we got a place to pitch the tents, each a free muffin, a hot shower and it was again our lucky day: It was pizza evening at the camp! A German woman who lived in the area made us all these yummy fresh pizzas from scratch. It was heaven!

The day we walked into Havelock felt like a change was lying ahead. There were plenty of new TA faces, with them came new stories and characters, and by then I had started to contemplate whether it was worth it for me to keep on walking in pain. I had missed a lot of tiny parts of the trail on the North Island, while trying to keep up with the team, and whenever there had been a section where it was possible to get a lift, I had gotten one to still be able to be with my Trail Family. But the Richmond Ranges were ahead; alpine crossings and about seven or eight days without civilisation. How worth was it, to limp it in pain, with a stiff ankle, and how safe?

Julia had gotten herself a room in a hostel in Havelock and we decided to stay there, too. Everyone resupplied in the small store and I had gotten myself, for me, the worst food ever. Lots of nuts and dried fruit, lots of muesli bars and chocolates, it was bulky and heavy and still I had the feeling it was too little for all those days in the wild. In the evening Julia and I had a tough goodbye and she decided to stay in the hostel for New Year's.

Stinky was fully packed, up to the top, the next morning and with time pressure from the Kiwis' schedule, we all had to hitchhike to Pelorus Bridge. I had started to work on getting a lift on the side of the main road and watched René and Rick walking towards me. I slit my eyes, looked at them and valued my chances "Me by myself will be fine. But chances will be limited if I had a Santa and a Chipmunk with me!" "You stay over there; don't you move closer to me. I am at work!" I told them off, in a friendly way of course, put out the thumb and scored a lift. "Byyyeeee" I shouted and "Good Luck" and off I was.

The guy dropped me off at the super busy Pelorus Bridge.

Pelorus River is popular for its beautiful swimming holes and clear water. It had drawn attention on itself, when Peter Jackson's "The Hobbit" took parts of the river on, for when the dwarfs escape the elf prison in the wooden wine barrels.

Mike and another German girl had hitched earlier the morning, I saw them at the cafe at Pelorus, but didn't feel like joining up with them, I did my own thing and started limping.

Pain, Pain and Pain for two kilometers on a road until I realised that I didn't want to walk on a gravel road for a few hours with this aching ankle. I was lucky enough to catch a lift out of the blue, by a gay German couple, who was on a holiday in New Zealand. They smelled like flowers. Stinky and I again just smelled ugly.

The two were lovely, but we didn't have much in common. They already missed cultural highlights like museums, concerts or exhibitions like they had back at home in Berlin. They missed market squares and proper town centers, but they dearly enjoyed the nature here.

Of course, I happened to be the first of the Crew, reaching Captain's Creek Hut. It was boiling hot, I had a swim in one of the swimming holes along the way, which was amazing and refreshing AND it was a trap; as soon as I had left the water I got attacked by murderous sand flies in thousands. In one second my legs were covered with little dark spots, attacking my skin with their little teeth. Fun police!

It was hard to do the 'Sandfly Dance' with a sore body part, my ankle, on little rolling river rocks. For the ones asking: "How does the 'Sandfly Dance' look like?" Please, youtube the Bavarian "Schuhplattler", speed it up times 10 and add another 20 moves with waving arms and legs to it. Just to get an idea...

I did escape in the end. But the bite marks remained for weeks.

It was the 31st of December, and we would have New Year's Eve out in the bush. Mike, René, Rick, Maud and Guillaume, Luca and I, we had a beautiful little bonfire and watched the stars appear in the sky. It was a great New Year's evening for someone like me who hated social events and who hated New Year's evening as much as I disliked Christmas.

With the new year eventually came the change. The morning of the 1st of January 2016, I finally was ready. I had made up my mind in the night and slept over it, so my thoughts were clear and rational. There was no way for me to go any further. I had dragged myself all the way into the bush to now realise that for nothing in this world I could carry on limping in pain.

I had harmed my body for too long, for too many kilometers and just couldn't bare the aches anymore. Tough decision. This time it was not for my Trail Family, this time it was for me.

I slowly started packing Stinky, silently being watched by René.

"What you doing?" he asked.

"I'm going back."

"Where back?"

"Back to Havelock. I can't walk any further."

"We can carry your gear."

"No, you can't."

"Will you have breakfast?"

"I'm going as soon as I've finished packing."

Again, I hated goodbyes. I wanted to make it as quickly as possible. All the times on the North Island, when I wished for being by myself, all that, made me feel devastated now in the actual real goodbye moment.

René and Rick sent me off with two big hugs, I cried, and I swear, there were a few tears on Rick's side, too. The last time I looked back I saw René hugging Rick.

Moments of goodbyes are hard. Is it harder for the ones that leave or for the ones that are left behind? Who was who in that particular situation?

I don't know, and it broke my heart to leave them all. It broke my heart to walk all the way back to the car park from where I had walked in, the afternoon before. Returning on the same track felt defeating and I must have cried most of the time this morning. I cried for leaving the people I loved, I cried for my Te Araroa journey and I cried for the pain, that stopped me living my adventure.

But I knew it was the right thing to do, to walk out, back into civilisation.

Peter and Jill, a lovely elderly Kiwi couple, who had been out on a day hike with friends squeezed me in their car. We had a good chat and they distracted me as well as the fact that crying in front of strangers, is not the healthiest thing for keeping your dignity.

They took me all the way back to Havelock. And then I was alone.

"Change is good" I say

I pitched my tent on the campground and I hid from the world. I slept, I cried, I slept, I ate, I cried. I didn't leave it till the night, in the dark, and I cried again. I missed the trail, the people, I missed Rick and René. I felt amputated and empty. In only a few hours I had discovered the darkest moment on my journey.

It seemed like the only thing that was left over from my trail was Stinky, my gear and the tent, that gave me shelter in my depression. It was my shelter the next day as well.

And then it was on the female version of René, Mike and Rick to now look after me. The three women from Queen Charlotte Track, Marlies, Sandie and Sarah, had just set up their tents; they recognised mine and found me in tears. It was good to talk to them and to just let the tears come.

I needed a place to stay for a while. I couldn't just stay on the campground and pay for the site for weeks, or however long it would take for my ankle to get better, if at all. I wanted to still be as close to the trail as I could, to still feel it around me.

Sandie gave me a phone number of a friend in Nelson. Jocelyn. "She might be able to help." Right that very moment I didn't want to hear it. There was no way I'd go all the way to Nelson and leave the TA. I needed to be on the trail! With Sandie's friend's phone number I hid away in my tent, and an unexpected text from René, who had climbed a little spur to get cellphone coverage, made me cry again that evening.

Sarah had injured her knee just before Havelock but decided to at least try to walk and carry on. So, they did the next morning. And alone I was again, with Jocelyn's phone number.

But with a phone call from Maud in the late afternoon things changed. Guillaume had protested to carry on, he was fed up with forests and walking the trail. Maud had made the tough decision to bail and go to Nelson, to sort out new plans for their travels in New Zealand.

"Join us in Nelson. We booked you a room in a hostel. Be with us."

So, it was Nelson then! I packed the tent that had given me a safe home for the last nights and days and got a lift into Nelson from a young couple. She was German, he was a Kiwi. They had met while she was a Wwoofer (Willing Workers on Organic Farms) at his parent's place.

"Lucky her." I thought. "Found her Kiwi to keep." They were super lovely and drove me all the way to the hostel and dropped me off. Now, can you remember in the beginning that I didn't try to find Germans but rather escaped from them? This hostel was a German paradise! It seemed like all young Germans, who had come to New Zealand without their parents, had decided to move into the same place at once, to have one big party. Maybe one could compare it to a childish Oktoberfest, without Australians though!

After being forced off-trail, I only saw a mess in it, it was the worst hostel I had stayed in, my whole life, and what a shocking contrast to the TA life it was. I told the guy at the reception that I would rather pitch the tent outside if possible. There was no way I would sleep in this party house. Luckily, tucked away in the corner, I found Maud and Guillaume's tent and parked right next to them. We hugged, and it was great to be with people that understood that there was more out there than just partying.

We had our TA connection and with our mid-twenties we were just too old for that place. So, instead of wasting time there, we headed out into town and discovered Nelson, the outdoor shops and its little cafes, and we actually had a really cool time together even though it was the stop of the TA journey for all of us.

Maud and Guillaume decided after a couple of nights to carry on as Te Araroa section hikers, which was fine with Guillaume. They were fit and started to resupply. I was jealous. I wanted to do that, too. But I couldn't. In the last days there hadn't been any improvement to my ankle at all.

My friends left in the morning to do the Nelson Lakes part of Te Araroa Trail.

It sounds terrible, but I disgusted this hostel even more being by myself. Those travellers, they had no idea about New Zealand. I listened to teenagers bullshitting about wwoofing places and Kiwis, bullshitting about places they had been to, and seemingly they were super cool and independent, now that they were far away from home, yes, old enough to have parties in a hostel. Most of them, sadly, had no interest in the country but just in the fact of drinking alcohol and pairing up with the likes of themselves. I honestly was fed up. I had come too far to drown at this place. I texted Jocelyn and got the response straight away: "I can help. I'll come and pick you up!"

The gear was packed in no time and Jocelyn was there straight after.

She is a beauty of a soul, strong, female and independent. In the small driveway she quickly turned her car, being watched by all the young boys that just waited for a reason to tell their silly jokes about women and cars. "I'm a woman who can drive a car!" she said and made me smile.

Jocelyn was a teacher at a girls college in Nelson and owned a B'n'B in Tahunanui, just a few kilometers out of Nelson's town center. I got given a room in the house for free and swapped from TA hiker to part time Wwoofer, and in exchange for me staying as long as I needed, I learned the ABC of keeping a B'n'B clean and tidy.

For Jocelyn I worked in the garden, weeded the drive way and steps, I vacuum cleaned the rooms and ironed the sheets and pillow cases. Jocelyn showed me how to make up a bed properly once or twice and the next time I would do it by myself.

Mum would have been proud of me.

Jocelyn trusted me in every aspect and after only a few days at her place I felt home. It was great to have a shower and a bed every night.

While I was mending, she picked me up to go to the supermarket every now and then, to buy my food for the next few days. She took me "OP-Shopping", second-hand shopping is big in New Zealand and I loved the little bits and bobs and preloved clothes that one could find in those stores. If it wasn't for Stinky's small volume I probably would have bought stuff in every single one, we visited.

Being with Jocelyn was fun and she really took over the female part of my New Zealand journey. I had spent months and months walking with smelly, burping and sometimes (often!) farting guys and now I had to adapt to this power woman who even was a passionate dancer. Quite scary for the coordination dyslexic that I am.

Days passed, and I got into a daily selfcare ritual. Being a physio, I spent at least one hour a day working on my ankle pain "Robert".

"Call everything by its name!" and with the name of "Robert" I made it a close friend rather than an enemy. Robert got a daily massage and mobilisation, followed by easy, gentle strengthening exercises. Day after day. What he seemed to love most was working in the garden. He was less sore after pulling the weeds and also more flexible.

And in Nelson, I lived for the moments of when the Crew came out of the wild, to then listen to their stories and me telling them how much I missed them, and them telling me how much they missed me.

We had Sandie, Marlies and Sarah visiting in Nelson. Jocelyn picked them up as Sarah had to stop walking because of her knees. So, now they were here for a few days and even Nathalie, the Belgian thru-hiker I had met on the North Island, came for a visit after bubbly, chatty Sandie and I had toured around in the town center, looking for little obscure shops.

Sarah stayed while the others kept going and we had lovely catch ups every now and then. We met for lunches or for Jocelyn's house-cleaning party which didn't sound tempting first, but then actually was really fun. Thank goodness unlike Jocelyn's friends, I didn't have a whole house to clean, but only my cosy tent which took me only a few seconds.

I loved my summer in Tahunanui. I basically got forced out of my Te Araroa nutshell and met new people in the B'n'B, met friends of Jocelyn's, she took me and her dogs Kiri and Lizzy to the beach for swims and walks, and slowly I mended. The ankle got stronger, the pain got less, and I took one of the old bicycles, that stood in the garage, and went on little trips.

I was fit to cycle to the supermarket and I would push it back up the hill to Jocelyn's after. One morning I almost accidentally committed suicide when I ended up on the wrong side of the road in a roundabout, having René's voice in my head "Whatever happens, stay on the left!" surely helped afterwards. Slowly I became more independent again. With the bike I could do anything; in the afternoons I cycled to my designated little private swim area at the sea in Tahunanui, and crashed on the couch afterwards, while listening to familiar music that Mum used to listen to when we were on summer holidays.

Then, one day, I did a little bike ride around town and suddenly I felt ready to properly test ankle "Robert". I pushed the bike and walked for one kilometer and another two. I actually was pain free. The ankle was more mobile, the swelling had gone, the pain had disappeared.

That set the spark! My head was processing the info: If I could walk pain free here, then I could go back on the TA!

It took me a couple of days to feel comfy with the idea of leaving civilisation behind and heading back into the bush.

I told the news to the Crew. They were happy, they wanted me to join again in Hanmer Springs. Alba would join them as well after having had a few weeks with her family. I chatted with Alba. We both agreed we missed René calling us "Darling". We missed Rick saying "Hey Guys" in his own special way when he needed our attention for taking a photo. Sorry, Mike - we agreed to not have missed the snoring in the night.

The offer of joining my Trail Family again was tempting. I'd be safe with them, but I also got given a chance to finally do things my way.

Why would life separate me from the Crew, to then eventually walk with them again? Maybe that was the hint and opportunity to now try and walk by myself? Why should I join?

Trail Journal entry for Friday 15.01.2016, Day 97

Had beach walk with Jocelyn and the dogs Lizzy and Kiri, afterwards hot chocolate in a cafe, quick work at home and back to the beach for a swim. Robert is better, more mobile and almost no pain.
Talked to Rick and Alba. They want me to join them again, to skip the Richmond Ranges and Nelson Lakes. Do I want that? No!
It's really tricky, why can't I have both, the team and the Richmond Ranges?
No, it is time to make my own decisions now. I will walk by myself. Whether it is the right decision or not, I don't know yet.
Whether I am worried about the Richmond Ranges? Definitely!
I don't know if the ankle will be okay, but it is my way and my decision. Walk it, limp it, crawl it.
Go over, go under, go through.
Cry, smile and scream.
Enjoy it, hate it, love it. Live it!

Jocelyn, of course, encouraged me to go by myself. No men are needed on adventures!
I had a few more chats, telling my Trail Family that I was not coming back, and read René's last message "Join us whenever you like. Have fun!"
I felt super bad and hoped they would still like me with the decision I had made. All in all, I really had made up my mind. I was going to do it alone, starting back at the same spot where I had felt so defeated and helpless, almost one month ago. Jocelyn would drop me off at Pelorus River in a few days.
Still I needed a backup plan. I had been injured and I had to grow my confidence in my body again. So, I planned on 10 days instead of eight for the Richmond Ranges.
Every day I got a few things from the supermarket and I resupplied different now. I weighed food for each day; snacks and breakfast were separately packed in little ziplock bags to help me stick to my food intake per day. I was not the best in being strict with eating my food, if there was

a bar of chocolate, then I would eat it in one go, not in little rows. Therefore, the "daily ziplock bag order" would help with that, and I also made another change: Having learned that Methylated Spirits can poison you and is heavy to carry, I finally bought myself a new stove and a gas canister. Now I was ready to hit the trail again!

For my last night in Nelson, Jocelyn took me to her partner Trevor's place on Best Island. A beautiful slice of paradise. It was a bach, and from the garden one could overlook the sea and overlook Nelson's waterfront in the distance. I had a wonderful evening and I almost couldn't sleep, knowing I would be back on the trail just the day after again.

We had a quick breakfast, took Kiri, the dog, and picked up a friend of Jocelyn's on the way. The drive into the Pelorus Sound was rather quiet.

I was too excited. I, too much looked forward to a walk in the woods again. We got out of the car and I took my first steps back on the TA with the best company one could have and finally we reached the junction on the track. Robert had kept quiet and was fine, I was relieved.

Big hugs and a thank you to Jocelyn, and our ways parted. The three walked back to the car and I walked up the familiar track that I was walking for the third time now. But on the 21st of January the direction was the right one. Onward to Bluff!

Home is where the Trail is

It was one of the best days on the trail. I was back in the bush, I could smell the trees and the warm, sweet smell of the soil, I heard the birds and the river. It felt like it was only yesterday that I was on the same track, with a group of people walking behind me, catching up once the hut was reached. In fact, it was over three weeks that I had left the Crew and bailed to heal my body.

The most important days on the trail were the days filled with emotions, this day was both, full of joy to be back, and full of grief for the team.

It took me a while to get into the hiking mode and once I reached Captain Creeks Hut, the hut, where we all said our goodbyes, I contemplated "Do I want to go there and stay there again? Do I feel tired or good? Do I really want to go back to a place that left such painful memories?"

I did, but only for five minutes. I left my name and intentions in the hut book and read the pages backwards to my entry on the 1st of January.

So many hikers had passed, so many people and names I didn't know and never heard of, unfamiliar names and unknown faces. Our Crew was something very special. We had walked together over months, whereas normally people just come for a few days and then go their own paths again. I think our connection was different and more profound than just to split ways on the trail and in life.

Now, that I was by myself, without my beloved Trail Family, I didn't feel like joining anyone anymore. No one could have reached the bond that we had.

Physically I felt really good that day and just carried on to Middy Hut. Knowing that it would be likely to have people behind me I didn't move into the hut but pitched my tent. I was solo, and I wanted to be solo.

Three Kiwis from Auckland and Friedemann "Peace-e" from Germany and a few more arrived after I did. I liked Peace-e, he was a young fresh character, but those Kiwis sadly didn't do any justice to MY Kiwis. It was too fresh, and I missed them too much to not to compare them to others.

We all had a chat, and the conversations got reduced to the topics gear, food, Te Araroa, aches and pains and the thru-hikers' mutual enemies, the sandflies. It was great to talk "Trail" again.

That night, I was happy to be back.

Trail Journal entry for Thursday 21.01.16, Day 103

WOW! I am back on Te Araroa Trail!
I feel so insecure and new but soooo happy to be here in the bush.
It's like coming home, from civilisation back into the jungle.
Like the guy in the Jumanji movie! I am home! I am back in my tent!
I have bush, birds and cicadas, as well as the sound of the Pelorus River.
So, so, so grateful!
Thank you! Thank you! Thank you!

A Kereru (NZ wood pigeon) welcoming me back on the trail

I slept well in the night, by the river, in my tent. I was back and yes, I was home! The next day everyone left before I did.

For some reason the manner of many thru-hikers is to do as many kilometers as possible a day. Everyone is focused on doing the 'Ks'.

I gave the others time to walk ahead to not bump into them again.

Rocks Hut was three hours away and as I had a first long day yesterday, I promised ankle Robert to get a short day today. We lived on compromises; long day, short day, long day, short day!

I had all time in the world as I had planned on taking 10 days for the section into St. Arnaud. Even though Stinky was super heavy, and probably tortured Robert step by step, we all got on well and it was great to know, that with the supplies I carried, I could easily do those 10 days or even more, if shit hit the fan.

The climb up to Rocks was alright, I remembered from reading René's online blog that they all struggled in the heat of the day. For me, in the late morning, not much of a problem. I reached Rocks Hut just after lunch time. A flash hut with flushing toilets. Now, that is something very weird to see in the bush, as normally it's just a more or less smelly long drop toilet with massive hungry blowflies that waited for their meal of the day. One poop to rule them all! One pee to find them!

Here at Rocks I had to check twice whether I had pushed the flush or not. The hut was cosy, and I hoped to be by myself for the afternoon and night.

Wrong. I had a day hiker visiting, unwrapping a massive pizza for lunch. He was lucky; I was still well fed from the stay in Nelson and didn't have any cravings, but a few weeks earlier and I would have killed him like a hungry Grizzly Bear his prey!

Wilbur from England and Liz a Canadian girl reached the hut and they just didn't seem to be in a hurry. Liz was bubbly and funny, we had a good time. Wilbur carried on after lunch. The two would meet again somewhere on the track.

Liz was the one to stay for a long time, we just got on very well, and by the time she left around 6pm, she was one of the contacts you make on a trail, but never see them again. From that on, I always walked behind her, reading her name in the hut books and once or twice she left a little note for me.

Short day, long day. Yes, what a long day I had, the next day. Not distance wise, but in hours and partly by choice. A nap in Browning Hut and a long chat with day hikers, several swims in a stream and a great hair and body wash in the afternoon made me reach Hacket Hut fresh and only sort of smelly. Shame about the hut, though; there was an old guy living in it. Hacket was close to a road end, therefore easy accessible for the public, and he just got in and out for resupplies, but had stayed here for already over two weeks or so. He was friendly but a little creepy, and he had these little anti mosquito smoke thingies to light in the hut which basically filled and thickened the air like having your head stuck in a plastic bag full of cigarette smoke. It was 10pm when I escaped and pitched my tent outside.

The next two days were epic with a steady climb up to the bush line and walking further to Slaty Hut on the tops as I planned on having my 25th Birthday on the top of the Richmond Ranges: Little Rintoul and Mt Rintoul. On the 25th of January, Rintoul Hut was a good eight hours walk away. It was the perfect day for being out in the open with sunshine and blue sky. The ridge line towards the mountains themselves was quite gentle and the views were to die for. I felt great, I was in good condition and then, with Little Rintoul, came the first defeat. It was boiling hot and it was a climb to die on as well. I puffed like a steam boiler and the sweat just ran off, I had a soaked shirt and the water ran down my back and into my shorts. The heavy, lazy carcass of Stinky didn't help with the climb either.

I got to the summit eventually, hugged the little orange pole, took some pictures and turned towards Mt Rintoul. Surely the beast of a mountain over there wasn't the one I was meant to go. "There is no way they make you go that steeply down to make you go back up that steeply again. That's a joke." To my disgust the track actually went there, you could see the little path dropping hundreds of meters and climbing up even higher, up to Mount Rintoul, on the other side of the dip. Now I had two options: I either walked. Or sat down and died.

It was a slippery slide going down Little Rintoul, recalling Sandie's and Marlies's text message back in Nelson, it almost "freaked them out." And it almost freaked me out! My feet couldn't find one stable grip in the scree and rocks, my boots pushed the stones down into the gully and I saw them disappearing in the tree line. If the stones could roll down there, then it was possible for a human being to roll down there, too.

In a moment of losing my feet I landed on my butt and securely slid a few meters further down. Awesome! Why not do the "Butt Slide" a little longer? With half of my body already on the ground I couldn't fall far, and I'd protect my knees from injuries. So, there I sat, slid down the narrow bits of the path and eventually made it to an even part.

If there would have been people with me, I guess I would have definitely lost my dignity that very moment.

I needed a little rest; a bigger boulder gave me shade and a little boulder for my scratched bottom was a fantastic opportunity for a seat. I took a sip of water and a little bite to eat, had a look back to the "thing" I had just maneuvered my body down from, and then I had a big, fat, decent cry for how stupid one must be to actually expose themselves on a trail like that and how silly of me to desperately wanting to be back on Te Araroa

Trail. I could have stayed in sunny, safe Nelson with Jocelyn and the B'n'B. I could have just become a normal traveller, sitting in a bus with other young people and only visiting the really famous and popular places of New Zealand, safe and sound in a hostel and in civilisation. Instead I had chosen to almost kill myself on a mountain, on my birthday.

"How awesome my gravestone would look like" I thought:

"Born 25.1.1991"

"Died 25.1.2016"

"Tumbled down the mountain, now hugging the trees forever."

Nevertheless, the cry was followed by "Shut the fuck up and walk the shit."

Mount Rintoul himself was a beast and a really fair climb, but it was actually enjoyable. The views from the tops were literally to die for again. I can't think of a better place to have a birthday party anywhere else than on 1731 meters in the Richmond Ranges.

The fun lasted until the descend. It was a sheer 500 meters drop down into the forest. I could see Rintoul Hut from the tops, telling myself that I'd be there in no time and that the worst was over. Go figure! That was not a track, that was scree slope sliding par excellence. Oh, I wished I was a little boulder to just quickly roll down there.

In good manners I started to slide on my feet, zigzagging down the slope, trying to keep my body upright, until the knees just gave way under the constant pressure. They just locked up and neither bending nor straightening worked anymore.

Good old "Butt Sliding Technique" worked wonders instead. I don't know if I can claim that piece of track to have walked, but I surely covered the distance with my body. A 200-meter constant butt slide was probably never seen before.

I actually walked the last piece to the hut, met a guy on his way up to cowboy camp somewhere on the tops, and got to my destination with the last drop of water in my bottle. What an awesome day it had been. I had birthday lollies and a yummy instant noodles dinner with a bit of cellphone reception, just enough to text my parents, and all that summed up a glorious birthday to remember.

Happy Birthday to me, Happy Birthday to me!

Another guy that I had met on the Pelorus a few days earlier caught up again. He had spent a few days in Nelson and was now back to meet his friend somewhere after the Richmond Ranges. I hiked with him the next day, followed him stupidly on a wrong track that had not been maintained for years and we bush bashed for something that felt like hours back to the right track. "What happens in the forest stays in the forest." but being alone in the wild sometimes does funny things to you and your mind.

I didn't feel a 100% well having him around. I encouraged him to hike further than Tarn Hut, even though he was tired, but eventually he left, and I had Tarn Hut to myself.

This very moment I felt lonely, I missed the humble and loving care of my Kiwis and read their hut book entry over and over again, just to get the feeling of having them right here. I wished to suddenly hear their voices outside, wished to suddenly have them stepping through the door, but of course that was not the case. They were miles away ahead of me.

With the buzzing company of friendly, curious bumble bees, I stayed in Tarn Hut for a Zero Day. Tarn Hut was a cosy place to be. The nights were entertained by a thousand of singing frogs and the wood burner was a great friend to dry wet stuff. Silly me accidentally burned a massive hole in my sock. Easy to be fixed that was!

I had purchased the socks in Kerikeri together with my boots, and after having had its surgery, stitched together with colourful yarn, "Frankensock" was the most beautiful, authentic sock ever, he surprisingly walked and lasted a fair mileage after that.

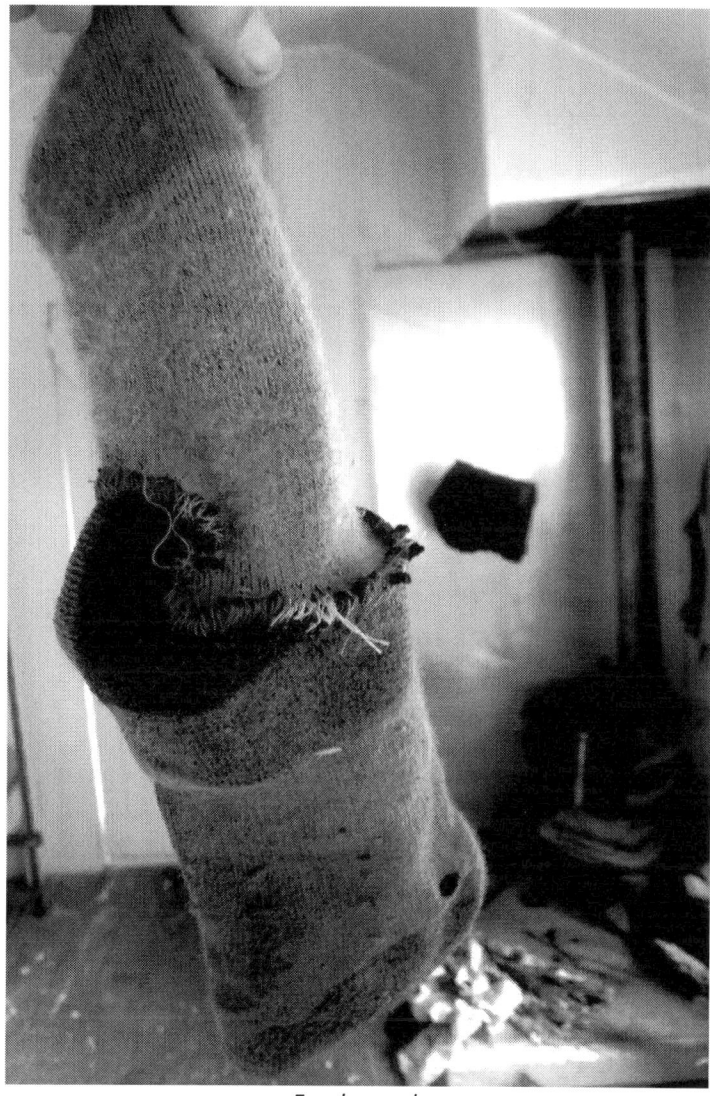

Frankensock

I left late to Mid Wairoa Hut the following day, had a refreshing dip in the clear blue waterhole close by, shaved my legs and armpits, cut my nails, brushed my teeth, brushed my hair and washed my undies.

Clean TA hiker I was!

Robert the ankle had kept up all those days, never had given me grief, and it was time for bigger days, now that I got trust and confidence back into the foot that had given me pain for almost half of the North Island.

After having Zero'ed and Nero'ed ("nearly Zeroed") the last days I felt fresh and pushed on from Mid Wairoa Hut, had a swim on the way, had lunch at orange painted Top Wairoa Hut, checked my GPS location and looked up to the ridge and Mt Ellis on 1300 meters, that I would need to climb up. The sky was blue, there were a few white clouds and it was warm. No reason to not go further.

Rick, Mike and René had talked about how quickly weather can change in the mountains, but the Rintoul crossing was fine for me under the same conditions and I was confident that it would stay fine that day, too.

Hot and sweaty on the climb, I reached the top and saw the clouds rolling in. Fast. In no time, I suddenly was in a low cloud, followed the orange poles and counted myself lucky to still be able to see at least two of them ahead. One of them ahead! None of them ahead! In less than 10 minutes my sight was reduced to five or 10 meters, white out, I was trapped in the cloud. I stood by the last pole I had found, and it slowly got cold.

I guess if people have never been in a situation like that they probably wouldn't believe how all of a sudden, a warm and sunny day could turn to custard in only a few minutes. I always thought it would happen slowly, with time to react, but there was no time for anything. I honestly didn't think of putting on more layers of clothing, which would have been the right choice at first. I only thought of getting out of that as quickly as possible.

On the whole journey, I was never more grateful for my cellphone and my GPS than in that very moment. By experience, I knew it would take ages to find my location, as it always did, sometimes 10 minutes depending on where I was, but here right now, in that moment, it was bang on spot.

No minute and the little blue dot appeared on the map, guiding me from pole to pole to pole. Step by step, meter by meter. It's accuracy honestly surprised me. My cellphone, the GPS and I, a team in the clouds.

As soon as I hit the tree line again I found shelter from the low cloud in the trees, found visible markers, and with the TA having a surprise behind every corner, whether a good or a bad one, a vista appeared after walking another kilometer, overlooking a big valley, a river, and Hunters Hut in the far distance. It was beautiful. I found a lovely campsite above the river before Hunters and called it my home for the night.

The landscapes in the Richmond Ranges are just stunning. Every day seems to be on a different terrain. Beech forest, exposed ridges and mountains, soft ground, hard ground, rivers, valleys, grass, rock, everything, you name it. Every day I loved the Richmonds a bit better.
I was healthy, strong, had no time pressure, had enough food to be able to stop when I wanted and was the maker of my day, with only my rules to follow.
I passed Hunters Hut the next morning, had a long break by a river, a clothes-wash and a bumblebee incident. That poor insect got trapped in my undies and scared to death in the particular moment of me putting them back on again. An 'ouchy'-moment for me. I don't blame you Mr. Bumblebee, I don't blame you.
I carried on to Porters Creek Hut, another orange painted hut that you could see from far away and made it my last stop in the Richmond Ranges. I would be out, back in civilisation after more than nine days, tomorrow evening. My head and tummy were fantasising over what food I would eat. Pizza? Cold fizzy drink? Cake? Cheese? Pie? Chips? Beer?
Even though I absolutely enjoyed walking the Richmond Ranges like a snail and loved being out in the wild, the excitement of reaching a town was unbeatable.
As I had to buy and pack smart for this long trip I only had wraps, peanut butter and honey for lunch, and after only five days already, there was no enjoyment in eating that anymore. I craved real food.
St. Arnaud, you temptress of a town - I just couldn't fall asleep that night!
Up at sparrow's fart, I had a long day on the track and then another 11 kilometers on the road into St. Arnaud. The track flew by, another beautiful day in the ranges, again different landscapes, with this epic tussock walk right at the end towards the safe travelling on a gravel road into civilisation. I popped out on State Highway 63 and faced the last 11 kilometers on tarseal. Again, feet don't have a big memory; after many days on natural ground the familiar darkness of concrete roads did beat the hell out of the feet at the end of the day. The kilometers were a challenge but the call of pizza, a shower, a bed and a Zero Day was strong. Cyclists, a few kilometers before St. Arnaud cheered me on "Go girl. Walking the TA. Good on ya", and from what I last remember is: Feet got freed, legs got lifted, a bottle of Sprite was opened, and a large Pizza didn't get to see the next day. Oh, what a glorious feeling! What an

achievement it was for me, the one that only walked by herself on 90 Mile Beach and from that on with a group of people, now finishing off what is supposedly the hardest part of Te Araroa Trail by herself.

Walking alone was quiet, it was challenging, it was boring and hard, it was intense in every way. I loved it!

I was definitely back on the trail after having had those three weeks off to heal my injury. Now I was in St. Arnaud and I needed people to celebrate with me. The Crew by then, was in the wild. A guy on a Harley Davidson would do; he had stopped for a break on the way through. I told him my story of conquering the hills, he had a look at my almost freshly shaved legs from three days ago, called me funny and drove off.

I spent the Zero Day with lying in, catching up on social media and worldly news, and later in the day caught a lift together with German girl Nina into Richmond by Nelson, for resupplying for the Nelson Lakes part. After shopping in town, we were lucky enough to be picked up in the early evening by a Dutch guy, who loved driving is car around and that didn't even need to go to St. Arnaud, but as it was "only" 25kms off the main road he decided to just drive us there. Awesome!

I prepared Stinky for the next days in the wild and just out of interest I checked René's online blog to see how the Crew was doing on their journey. Their schedule showed Wanaka for the 9th of February, only a few days away. If I wanted to see them again before Bluff, then Wanaka would be the only option.

It would take me about eight days to do the section in the speed I was going, and I didn't want to feel rushed. I would see how I went the next days and either try to meet up with them, or maybe not.

A little Mission

The walk to Lake Head Hut was only a short one, I had left St. Arnaud late, took a picture of the famous jetty by Lake Rotoiti, had two swims along the way and got to the hut in the early evening. I had a lovely hut night with Louise from Sweden and Rinse from the Netherlands, who were on the Travers Sabine Circuit, and Imme from Denmark, who was also walking the TA.

I spent half the next day walking with Louise, who caught up to me sometime after lunch at John Tait Hut. We followed the track along the river, through beautiful dense bush and eventually gradually climbed up towards Upper Travers Hut, that is surrounded by rugged mountain ridges and Travers Saddle, which we had to climb up the next morning.

I really loved being with Louise, Rinse and Imme. All were fun hanging with and as Louise noticed "so ordinary and so normal" as she had expected people that do long-distance hikes to be more like Superman and Superwoman, rather than two average girls like Imme and I.

The next morning, the four of us solved the mystery of "who was the person that walked through our bunk room in the night and that scared the hell out of us all?" Was it the Travers spirit? Or a confused wild human that hid in the area, sneaking people's food? Or was it one of the German couple that slept in the other room?! There was denial on the German couple's side with eventually the woman confessing that she had "gotten lost in the night on the way to the long drop."

The track climbed up over Travers Saddle, big boulders had to be climbed which made ascending fairly quick and with every step one was a meter higher than before. It flattened out on the top and continued as a route down into a river valley. Low clouds were hanging in the hills, but the valley I headed to, several hundred meters below, was still visible. The route dropped steeply, over avalanche risk areas, into gullies full of scree. Zigzagging was the only way to sort of keep the knees sane. The Tararuas and Richmond Ranges had taken their toll on my knees, and the longer I kept walking on the TA the sooner and more frequent they started screaming on a downhill section. It felt endless on this descend. I passed people climbing up, wished I could go uphill, too, but continued to drop steadily. The track then headed into the trees and finally popped out by the river. I cooled down my ankles and knees in the first bigger stream I crossed and had first lunch.

Rinse was the first to catch up and together we walked to West Sabine Hut. The track was easy to follow, there was a beautiful gorge that we crossed on a bridge, we had second lunch in the hut and Rinse took off. Left alone, quite happy to walk by myself, I carried on shortly after him.

It was another three hours to Blue Lake Hut, I already had about six or eight hours in the legs but felt okay to walk the next stretch, especially as the weather forecast didn't look too tempting for the next day. I was better off sitting the weather out in Blue Lake Hut before approaching the "Nelson-Lake-Monster-Climb" up to Waiau Pass, that would take place shortly after Blue Lake.

The track climbed and followed a stream, changed from gentle and wide to narrow and steep and eventually sidled along a raging river full of gorges. The water so blue and clear, it's hard to imagine; so refreshing looking, so tempting to drink and touch, while on that sweaty rugged climb towards the lake. The last meters felt like ages. I got tired and ran out of energy, had a long break before reaching the hut and happily stripped of my boots and socks once I got there.

A possum had died in the water tank and it was not recommended to drink from the tap, but to get drinking water from Blue Lake instead.

This was one of the purest waters I had ever seen. The ground of the lake visible, and trees and mountains got reflected in the strong blue of the lake. Such a special place is so worth protecting. DOC had put up signs recommending and asking people to not swim in the lake, to not pitch tents near the lake, to not wash dishes in there as well as making use of the long drops rather than pooping close to it. I sadly doubt that some people care. We already had people up there pitching the tents on the lake shore and later on I heard people talking about how wonderful it was to swim in it. Poor Blue Lake. Such a popular side trip on the Travers Sabine Circuit already and now, with the increasing popularity of Te Araroa Trail, so exposed to humans and their waste.

Eventually I got my fresh water from the stream running out of the lake and as I never cleaned my pots anyway, I didn't even come close to touching the lake.

Later in the evening we finally met those Supermen and Superwomen, Louise was talking about. Four American thru-hikers popped in.

No "Hello" to us hikers in the hut. They only called each other by their trail names, they had gotten from probably walking the Appalachian Trail or Pacific Crest Trail in the States. They ignored the weather forecast for the next day, had to do their 40 kilometers per day to be acknowledged as awesome demi-god thru-hikers and even the DOC recommendation to not attempt crossing Waiau Pass in bad weather was ignored.

They were "Ultralights!" It is a certain trend and hiking style in the United States where people try to wear and carry the lightest and simplest gear only, to then be able to walk longer and faster. The base weight (the weight of the tent, sleeping bag, tent, backpack and sleeping mat) of Ultralights often only reaches between four to five kilograms, which eventually sums up to roughly 10kg or even less, once they add a few lightweight clothes, some water, food, and other stuff. In comparison, average backpackers are likely to carry between 14 and over 20 kilos on their backs. How safe and prepared those ultralight-hikers are in cold and wet conditions in the mountains is questionable.

Our four 'Ultras' carried on in the morning with low cloud and rain, never to be seen again. We "kids" nevertheless had an awesome Zero Day at Blue Lake, listened to the howling wind and rain on the roof in the morning, had a play-around Blue Lake, once the rain had stopped in the early evening and just had a good time.

We said our goodbyes the next morning with a beautiful blue sky.

I left early. Now I was on a mission! I just had to do it: I had to be out in two and a half days to get to Wanaka to meet the Crew on the 9th of February.

A rugged thing Waiau Pass was, already the approach route could have easily made you slip and fall into Lake Constance, but climbing up this pass was hard, hard, physical work. Gently it started to climb and suddenly I ended up on the familiar slippery scree.

New Zealand's alpine tracks love the scree!

One step up meant slipping two steps back down. Not helpful when you're trying to make progress. With one step at a time and focusing only on the very next marker, I gradually 'snailed' my way up towards the pass. Every now and then I just had to turn around and gaze over the alpine valley below, as well as Lake Constance's big moraine wall and the distance I had covered. I reached the marker on the top of the pass, celebrated with myself, took pictures, had a quick snack and just admired the views and the achievement.

Just a la Te Araroa Trail it first made you walk up, to then let you drop down steeply into the next valley again. It was a steep boulder climb in parts. Surprisingly I really enjoyed the action it involved. While descending, my athletic moves reached from Spiderman imitations to 'Butt-Slide-Girl'.

Rugged Nelson Lakes

Soon after, I dropped into the next valley, all by myself, no one else there, just me, the mountains and majestic waterfalls. I had a trail shower in a stream. Washed hair and body and was ready and refreshed to carry on for another few hours. I passed lovely camp spots along the way, which I had probably considered to be a place to stay if I hadn't been on my little mission. I just missed my friends! I missed their voices, I wanted to hear their stories and I wanted to tell mine.

The track slowly levelled out and changed into an easy walk in a wide, broad river valley. I reached Caroline Bivvy in the early evening. It is a two-bunk shelter by the river, and I only stopped to have a quick chat with a man and his boy, out on a weekend trip, but that was enough time to attract hundreds of sandflies in the size of blow flies. They were hungry vicious beasts. The worst spot to stay and the worst sandfly spot I had discovered so far. Pelorus River in the beginning of the Richmond Ranges was nothing compared to that massacre. Quickly I left a note in the intentions book and ran off.

I spent the next day walking in boiling heat. It was a long day on the flats, easy walking and great to cover big distances, but as the day continued, the heat got unbearable and the sun shone on me without any mercy.

I had to make it to Boyle Village by lunchtime the day after, if I wanted to make it to Wanaka in the evening. Therefore, I had to do kilometers now and suck it up. The more I would walk today, the less I had to walk tomorrow, and the more time I would have to hitch along the West Coast. My legs carried me past Anne Hut and I puffed up Anne Saddle, I carried on until after 6pm and I wanted to stop at Rokeby Hut for the night.

By the time I got to the last stream crossing, before the two-bunker, my brain got dizzy and I felt weak. My face was burned, and my body was exhausted from sweating for hours on end. I swear I felt like lying down on the ground and collapsing right where I stood.

Had I drunken enough water today? Had I eaten enough?

I sat by the stream, filled my water bottle, slowly drank little sips from it, had a little snack and after that I made it to Rokeby Hut to pitch my tent among the trees, as the bunks were already occupied by section hikers.

I only had water for dinner that night, food just didn't want to go down. Funnily enough the next day I felt fit like never. I had been almost dead and dried out, wrinkly like a raisin in the evening before, but now I felt like a newborn juicy grape.

The kilometers to Boyle Village just flew by. I made it to the intentions book and signed myself off "Leaving the TA for a while, for a family holiday."

Family Affairs

Proud as one can be about making it to Boyle early enough, I quickly gobbled food and went to 'work'. I wanted to catch my Trail Family and I had to cover more than 600 kilometers with hitchhiking. If I had had a car it would have been seven hours of a drive, without a break, but I was on foot and only had my thumb to get a lift.

Lucky me scored one straight away. It was an elderly couple, who were on their way to Hokitika on the West Coast. Score! The two smelled beautifully clean. I smelled like a public toilet.

We stopped for ice cream on the way and it was like being their granddaughter; they just looked after me. While passing the farmlands, the woman pointed out the farm houses on the sides of the road, "Aaah, he doesn't love his wife enough!" she said whenever we passed a small house. "Here, he must love his wife!" she said when we passed bigger ones.

"Maybe the one with the little house loves his wife more." I thought "Less space to clutter and collect things, less bathrooms to clean as well."

I guess the definition and understanding of "Love" is different from person to person. For me Love is spending time with people I like. Like my Te Araroa Family, who were about to reach Wanaka either today or tomorrow.

My elderly helpers dropped me off in Hokitika and further I got with a couple, who were travelling around the West Coast. Everything on my hitchhike mission went smooth. On the way I texted Rick to let him know that I was safe and sound in Boyle Village, just to make sure, for once and for all, that they would not see me again, so that the surprise would be even more unexpected. The Crew must have been out of cellphone coverage as there was no response from his side.

Thumb out and off I was again. I was in a hitchhike rush until I reached Fox Glacier. It started to get late, it was almost 6pm and I set the line for 7pm. Once it would turn 7pm I would stop hitchhiking and would find a place for the night. Still I had almost 300 kilometers ahead. I could see me failing. It turned 6:15pm and no one picked me up. It turned 6:45pm, and I just stuffed my last wrap with chocolate in my mouth, when a car pulled over.

"Where do you want to go?" a guy with a Spanish accent asked me. "Wanaka" I mumbled, still with the chocolate wrap hanging out of my mouth.

"I go there. Jump in!"

My eyes almost popped out and I almost choked on my food.

It was 6:50pm when Mr. Spanish guy and I left Fox. I had a super enjoyable time and a great chat with this trail angel, still, felt a bit sorry for him, as he had to put up with my strong smell for around four hours, though. Maybe that was the reason why he sometimes stopped along the way, to quickly get out of his car and take pictures of landscapes?

By the time we reached Wanaka, it was around 10pm and Mr. Spanish guy, alias Alejandro, dropped me off at the campground. I pitched the tent and wrote my journal. What a day that was! So many kilometers I had done. It must have taken me 10 hours or more to get here plus with the hours I had walked this morning it was a hell of a day. Then I fell asleep.

I was excited came the next day. The Crew would be so close now. Regarding their schedule they would walk into Wanaka from Albert Town, a short day for them.

I mucked around in the morning, sorted my washing, paid for the tent site, had a quick shower to look clean and smell good, or at least not like a walking rubbish tip, and then I slowly started to walk around the lake towards Albert Town. I found a hidden place off the lake track on a big branch of a tree, where I could easily spy around the corner to see the Crew coming. I imagined the moment they would pass me, they wouldn't notice me on my branch, and I could just slowly creep behind them to eventually greet them. It would be awesome!

30 minutes passed, an hour went by, one and a half hours, I got nervous, did I read the schedule wrong??

I texted Alba. No response.

I texted Rick. Nothing.

I was starving on my branch, hadn't had any breakfast and didn't bring water with me. In desperation I called René.

"Daaarling!" he screamed into the phone.

"Where are you guys?" I asked.

"We're in a cafe in Wanaka."

"You're in a cafe in Wanaka?!" How the heck did that happen! How could I have missed them on that track?

"Darling. Where are you?" he yelled.

"I'm by the lake. On the track."

"Which lake?"

"Here. This lake. Lake Wanaka." I yelled back.

Almost starved to death on my branch, I climbed back down, headed back into Wanaka and found the Crew happily munching on pastries in a cafe at the lakefront.

The Crew in Wanaka

It was a superb moment, seeing those faces, how they had changed over the weeks and how wild they all looked now. All our hair was bleached from the sun, the boys' beards were big and looked like birds' nests.

Rick looked like Santa Claus more than ever before, and René's beard gave him even more chipmunky cheeks. Young Luca still desperately tried to grow a proper beard and lovely Alba looked gorgeous as ever.

Our skin was tanned from walking in the sun for weeks on end. We all had these funny body tans; once we took the boots off, after a long day, we would free the creatures that lived in the shadow. Those creatures were these cheesy, pasty feet that had wrinkles and looked like feet of dead bodies. In combination with our beautiful brown legs, the whole picture was just grotesque.

Poor little feet, here they are, doing all the hard work, and these little machines get punished for hours on end and yet, they never get to see the sunlight. I'd be protesting if I was a foot.

It must be like working in an office in wintertime. You leave the house in the dark, spend the day inside the office and you come home in the dark. Feet – I can feel for you guys!

I absolutely loved René's story about how women had spied on him on their Zero Day in the Hot Pools in Hanmer Springs. René had lost several kilos, he had the funny sock mark tan, and to top that, he had the fluffy beard. He said he really had to fight the daughters' mums off and protect himself from proposals. I get your point, you must have looked just....adorable.

In Wanaka, I had my Trail Family back. I had René back, Rick, Alba and Luca. No Mike. He had left the team to walk the TA by himself. Someone didn't like this schedule either. I can't blame you Mike and good on you!
Instead of Mike, we had Ray, a friend of René's again, joining for the Motatapu Track. We hugged a lot that afternoon and it felt like it was a great motivation for us all, to start the Motatapu section towards Arrowtown and Queenstown together. I would be walking this track together with the Crew again for the last time.
For the next days it would almost be like it was before we parted ways in the Richmond Ranges. We would have four days of Crew-Revival!
We all resupplied in town and had a great dinner. My shout for all.
A proper late birthday dinner for me.

Even though it felt like normal being with the team, something had changed. I was not this inexperienced German hiker anymore. I really was a grown-up hiker now. I had experienced Kiwi life in Nelson and had walked two of the hardest sections on the TA by myself. I had figured out my new resupply strategy and had my own rhythm and pace. My friends had theirs. In the mornings, I was a quick packer, I got up, had breakfast and would pack my things to make sure I got away early enough. I had become a snacker rather than a luncher, and I didn't take big lunch breaks anymore. On top of that, even though, I had had this long break due to my injury in Nelson, I actually was bloody fit. I had stopped eating too many sweets; I even didn't consume Snickers bars anymore and that meant I didn't carry a lot of sweet stuff, also I drank more water rather than eating food. With that I lost a couple of kilos myself and my body felt more endurable, leaner and fitter.
From Wanaka I started earlier than anyone else, had a long break for a swim and got over taken by the team. By the time I got to Fern Burn Hut they had already installed themselves. It was the nicest feeling to know they were in a hut with me.
Still I loved walking by myself but as I experienced in the Richmond Ranges, the loneliness in a backcountry hut can make you feel very isolated. So, here they were with me. I planted myself in between Rick and René for the night, and again I had the loving trusty feeling of my Trail Family around me, to feed my stray soul with.

The Motatapus were again a stunning part of Te Araroa Trail. We crossed Shania Twain country. The Canadian singer had bought the land and supported the building and renovation of several wonderful backcountry huts, so that trampers could use them. The Motatapus are purely tussock, it is not natural, but man made. Maori tribes used to hunt for food and on their way, they burned down the native bush.

We tourists see New Zealand's green rolling hills as a natural landscape and we walk or drive past them without rethinking what we see. Those green hills, one day, were native bush, before the human influence, by Maori and the English, changed New Zealand's environment dramatically. Instead of bush it is forestry, towns or dairy farms, that pollute the soil and affect the water quality. While we tourists enjoy '100% pure New Zealand' we don't always get or read the information. Happiness sometimes is just a lack of knowledge.

Also, there, I had to finally ditch my stitched-up "Frankensock" and his partner. I swapped them to a new pair of socks, and from that on the two were allowed to enjoy their retirement and travel in Stinky.

We popped down into the Arrow River valley, then followed the track into an old gold mining town called Macetown, which was first settled in the 1860s due to the discovery of gold in the Arrow River as well as its catchments. Later the miners focused on digging into the hills and once they failed finding gold, the village turned into a ghost town by the 1930s. The miners had failed, and I was about to lose the Crew.

I desperately needed to pee, hid behind bushes, and by the time I walked back on the track, everyone was gone. So, there I was walking by myself again. I had done it over the last weeks but now I felt left behind, I tried to speed up to catch them again but couldn't. I felt like an animal that got separated from the herd. It made me feel unsettled. A slight sign of a little trail-panic-attack forced me to reboot myself. What the heck was that now? Why would I, that had walked perfectly safe and confident by herself, now struggle and panic because she was without the team? What is different to walking behind a group of people to just walking by yourself? Human minds function in a funny way...

I slowly got back into my single walking mode and stopped feeling panicky, reminded myself of the days I had walked alone and that I was fine back then. From the track where I stood, I spotted a glimpse of René walking on a gravel road, then disappearing. They just took the road instead of the track. Wimps!

My track led me high up into the mountains, through ankle rolling tussock and my reward was a stunning view over the Queenstown-Wakatipu basin. All in all, it only took me a little while longer on my track than it took the team on the road. We met up in Arrowtown again.

Everyone pitched their tents on the campground, we had showers and went out for a well-deserved large pizza dinner.

On the last day with the Crew we walked into Frankton just before Queenstown. It was Chinese New Year's and the South Island metropolis is best not visited during that time, as it is packed with tourists. Everything was fully booked and the last unpowered tent sites in town were NZ$40 each; so, Frankton Motorcamp was the chosen place for the night instead. We shopped for dinner, cooked together and spent the last evening as a Trail Family. It was tempting to carry on with them; safe and sound with the Crew and the company of loved ones, it was almost like with the Germans back in Auckland – way too easy to get pulled into only hanging with them. I stayed in Frankton.

Saying goodbye was hard, letting them go after just being reunited again. But it felt right now, to just let it happen. It was a better and clearer goodbye than the one in the Richmond Ranges in January.

I now had my trail to go back to, they had to follow theirs. For them, the trail would be over in a few days. My trail still continued for longer. All adventures were ahead of me. It was my home, my journey, about 700 kilometers away. The stray had to return home.

Rolling Stone

I hitchhiked back to Wanaka, met up with Louise, who I had met on the Nelson Lakes part, and her friend Remco for the evening and then caught an Intercity Bus in the morning that brought me back to Franz Josef.

A hitch later I was in Hokitika, the weather had turned to custard and a storm was on the way. I had no rush to go on the trail as the rivers would have been flooded anyway. Instead I got offered to sleep in a campground's kitchen while the storm hit the West Coast with thunder, rain and heavy winds.

I hitched to Greymouth the next day, scored a lift with a Maori guy who hated tourists, but I was "okay" because I was a "walker."

"Thanks for that!" I thought and so didn't feel good in that car anymore.

Once in Reefton I only had to pass Boyle Village and I would be in Hanmer Springs. Back on the track.

I got picked up by this crazy grandma. She had saved up all her money to finally buy the love of her life: a black Mercedes Benz. She listened to rocky country music while I got tumbled around on the passenger seat when she hit the corners, then she accelerated out of the corners, and in my memory, she was the one that had a crazy grin on her face every time she could speed up her baby. Crazy Grandma Schumacher dropped me off at the intersection to Hanmer Springs and disappeared in a dust cloud down the road.

"Du ju wont tu go tu Haenmer Springs?" A German couple asked me once they had pulled over.

"Sis is not far, wie will taik ju sere."

"Great", I felt grateful for that, but avoided talking, to not expose me as a Landswoman, too.

Hanmer Springs was lovely, a good place for a rest, so I spent two nights there, to resupply and to soak in the Hot Pools. I actually only soaked for five minutes and realised it was too hot and that I obviously was not a soaker in summer time, as it made me feel dizzy, so instead I did my laps in the swimming pool. I resupplied in town for the next days into Arthur's Pass and with the next day I was ready to hit the trail again.

I had gotten a lift out of town and tried to get a lift back to Windy Point, just before Boyle Village, to connect with the TA. It was hard to get people to stop, I had waited for 30 minutes already and it got harder when suddenly two TA hikers turned up on the road. The girls were NOBOS, North Bounders, and had sat out the bad weather in Hanmer Springs as well. Now we were three people trying to get to our destination.

We waited another 20 minutes until we finally got a car to stop. In fact, it was a campervan full of older English people who were on a holiday in New Zealand. They were excited to see three girls with backpacks on the side of the road and gave us all a lift.

I was the first to get dropped off as the girls had to go into Boyle Village to walk north into St. Arnaud.

After all the rain the tracks were muddy, and my dry shoes got slightly damp after a few seconds. Nothing new on Te Araroa Trail, I can't remember that I once had dry shoes for more than three days in a row (Not even on 90 Mile Beach the shoes stayed dry). Usually they got wet the first minutes in a track and stayed wet until I hit a town again or when I had super-hot temperatures to dry them out. Wet shoes normally are accepted with a sigh of resignation, and one would just ignore the sloshing and squelching noises they made while walking.

That day I tried my best to not completely soak my shoes with water straight away and actually did really well until I saw Hope Kiwi Lodge in just 100 meters distance. Only a knee deep, slow flowing stream had to be crossed. Of course!

With wet feet I slogged towards Hope Kiwi Lodge, a fancy looking hut in a lovely valley. It had several separate bunk rooms and a big cooking area as well as a paddock for horses. In the hut were two hunters, they had been out in the bush for a decent time already. Lovely guys and reasonable about killing animals.

In most of the backcountry huts in New Zealand one would often find "Hunting Magazines", the front pages most often showed a smiling hunter proudly posing with a massive dead pig on the ground or a dead stag on the shoulders. The pictures inside were hardly different from that.

The magazines told stories about "Sport Hunting" and "Trophy Hunting", they showed all sorts of weapons and guns and gear that were available for hunters to buy. "Pure testosterone!" So basically, those magazines are the "Playboy" for hunters to do "Hunting Porn" in the time while they are inactive.

I totally understand and get that hunting is popular in New Zealand and that hunting is a form of pest control, as well. They shoot pigs, deer and goats that would just eat away the undergrowth and some hunters probably shoot possums on their way, too. Although, I never understood how people went "Trophy Hunting"; killing animals for fun and for fame and to eventually end up on the front pages of those magazines.

Those hunters in the hut nevertheless were animal stalkers; in all the days they had spent in the bush so far, they hadn't shot one animal. They just enjoyed watching the behaviour of deer and they loved being out in the bush, in the dawn of morning, to enjoy the silence until the bush woke up. When I arrived at Hope Kiwi Lodge the two just emptied packages of lollies and had a really good time.

That evening, Davorin walked into the hut. A Croatian, who partly lived in New Zealand, he had done the North Island TA a few years back and was now to walk the South Island part. He was a passionate photographer and his pack was old and worn, and with the camera gear, massive and probably really heavy. Davorin and I would from now on meet on and off, on the TA, for the next weeks as we both had the same rhythm. Both of us wanted to enjoy the trail, not rush it. We had the same distances and destinations in our heads and had about the same walking pace. From all the people I met after leaving my Trail Family, he was to be the closest of a trail-dad to me.

Gareth, a funny, chatty Kiwi guy, turned up later that day. He told everyone that he absolutely hated walking but had decided to walk the trail to raise funds for foster families and foster children.

We had a great evening, chatting about New Zealand's nature and society. While the guys went more into "men talk", I turned my attention towards the intentions book, found Rick's familiar writing and realised that I missed them nevertheless but had to now let them slowly go.

When I left Hope Kiwi Lodge in the early morning hours, I passed the hunters on their way back, without a deer or a goat, still the two had had an enjoyable time in the woods.

On this Te Araroa section I encountered the natural thermal pools, the trail notes had mentioned. While suffering from the heat of the day, I had run out of water and just reached a little waterfall, wanted to cool myself down and fill the bottles, but the water was warm, even hot. The sign for the TA Hot Pools, where you can soak for free! Davorin, I and an Italian section hiker, had a little bath. Mine only lasted three seconds; it was just too hot. I watched the water in the river below, how wonderfully cold and refreshing it must be.

The bush on our section over Harper Pass made me feel like being in a jungle; the water was so clear and cold, the bush itself dense and lush and the sandflies here reached the 2nd ranking of the worst beasties ever.

I crossed path with a stoat, that seemingly didn't expect humans, as it dropped its freshly caught little fish while panicking and took off. Davorin and Gareth told me later that they had seen it; the stoat had returned to its prey and had then disappeared into the undergrowth to have a feast.

It probably would have loved the dead, smelly feral cow that was just decomposing next to the river a few kilometers upstream as well.

Great for drinking water quality! How could cows end up here in the middle of nowhere anyway?!

Davorin and I met plenty of non-TA hikers on the saddle as well as DOC workers, who were out doing track maintenance, telling us that there were more DOC staff at Locke Stream Hut, only a few kilometers away.

Yip, they were! You could hear them having a great time. The music was going, the BBQ was on, there was beer and juice and yummy food. Doesn't that sound like the dream job ever? Out in the bush for a few days, plenty to eat, talking to hikers, listening to music, painting and maintaining a hut, bird songs,.........Out of a sudden job envy I decided to not to stay there that night and carried on further down the Taramakau valley, eventually found a cute tent spot under trees and covered myself in long johns, socks and long sleeve to fight off the massive blood sucking terror flies while eating my dinner. Fun police again!

What a beautiful day it had been. How content I felt that evening, how confident I was in the wild. I was happy.

Happy I was the next morning, even though I ended up being breakfast for the terror flies, I managed to escape without getting too anemic.

I eventually followed a four-wheel drive on the river flats and discovered two private huts on a clearing close to Taramakau River. Funnily enough one of the hunters I had met in Hope Kiwi Lodge poked his head through the door, waved at me and we had a quick chat.

I had read about this section of the TA in the trail notes and it made me worried as I had to cross the Taramakau shortly after that clearing. and I knew it was a big river. Afterwards the track would continue only as a route ergo "pick your own way." The hunter reassured me that the river would be fine to cross. He had done it yesterday and it was okay. Still I was super nervous. From all the things I feared the most on the TA was sheer impassable, steep landslips and river crossings. Rivers were the powerful untamed force that I had no control over and never will.

I took the track down to the river, I saw the wide river valley and heard the water rushing down. My tummy grumbled from nervousness and the sudden urge of visiting a toilet combined with belly cramps, got me ducking behind a big tree, digging a hole and covering the remains with stones.

Taramakau River was a beast. It had white-water rapids and the water hit bigger rocks in the river bed to make it look even more dreadful and hopeless to cross.

I had four options.

Option one: Waiting for Davorin, the Italian guy, Gareth or the group of people and to cross with them.

Option two: Turning around to go back to the hunter and ask him for help.

Option three: Crossing the river before the confluence and try to cross the other creek from the far side.

Option four: Sit down and have a decent cry.

As much as I loved option four, I was brave enough not to cry yet.

As much as I loved option one and two, I was silly enough not to sit and wait or turn around.

It was not the smartest of my ever-made decisions on the trail and it was one of the (a few weeks later) famous "well that was dumb moments" on my journey.

I tried to cross the river where my GPS told me, got in the water less than halfway and my legs and walking poles almost got pulled away. I turned around. "The river is fine to cross, my arse!" I cursed at the hunter almost picking option four that very moment.

After walking a few meters upstream, I tried again and succeeded. I had made it to the other side above the confluence. Now, I only had to cross the creek that came out of a valley ahead of me, and that separated me from the other side with only a few meters width. Upstream I had a really deep, slow flowing pool to cross. Downstream whitewater rapids were waiting to swallow a silly hiker with their deadly speed.

It was only a few little meters to the other side but with this water in between, unreachable. I just couldn't believe it.

Now option one, waiting for other hikers, would have probably been the smartest thing to do.

Stubbornly, all of a sudden, the pool became more and more attractive to me. No matter what, I had to reach the other side!

So, I secured all the things, that didn't like to get wet, in my drybags, unbuckled the belt of Stinky, took my poles and stepped into the water. First step - ankle deep, second step - calf deep, 5th step - knee deep, 7th step - hip deep, 9th step - belly button deep. I felt Stinky's bottom floating in the water while I pushed myself along. Two more meters. The force of the water in the pool was strong and I hadn't realised how much flow it really had until I was more than halfway. The other side so close and yet so far. One more meter and then I could feel the water leaving my belly button and the hips, it left the knees and the ankles, and I was on the other side. Blessed are the fools! I had made it in a moment of dumbness. I had crossed that beast by myself. I felt like the king! I had the silliest smile on my face, I took pictures of myself with a wet shirt and I cheered on a video for Mum, telling her about another "Liebe Mutti Moment" in a raging river. René would have been proud of me!

The adrenalin left my body within minutes, my legs started to shake, and I acknowledged that it was pure stupidity to have tried and crossed this river by myself. I could have died in there and no long-distance trail is worth dying for. For that, I felt a bit stink.

Still a few days later I sent the heroic video to Mum. I just couldn't help myself. Sorry Mum, I deeply apologise and swear I will never risk my life in a river ever again.

The last stretch that day was, what symbolised a lot of parts of the TA. "Pick your own track" ended up with bush bashing, little river crossings, sidling actions and the rarest moment of sighting an orange trail marker every now and then. Just enough to reassure that I was on the right path. From bad to worse!

Once upon a time....

...there was a young German girl, that was headed into the wilderness of a foreign country, to experience what walking a long-distance trail was like. She found her feet, made friends and she encountered the most beautiful landscapes she had ever seen in her life. She had found solitude and gained pride, she fought off dangerous, blood sucking monster flies, had crossed a wild river and in a moment of lack of attention, she passed the sign of Otira Flood Track....

The big spiderweb I ended up having glued to my face while bashing through a bush should have told me already that it was not a good idea to walk that track, but I was so damn close to Morrison's Footbridge, State Highway 73 and the safety of civilisation that I just ignored it. Maybe the next 10 spiderwebs should have made me rethink my plan, obviously no one had walked here for a while! At least I could have rechecked it with the trail notes. Then I would have read that this track had not been maintained for years and that it was not recommended to take, but if possible to cross Otira River instead.

The sign in the beginning had said two hours to the footbridge.

"Easy peasy."

I followed the markers, climbed steeply and descended steeply.

I scratched my legs, slipped and fell through the plants that had grown for years and balanced over a massive fallen tree three times because I had lost the trail markers. I jumped, and rock climbed, bush bashed and tried to find any vital signs of me being on the right track. Otira Flood Track almost brought me down to my knees. After two hours of desperately fighting against mother nature and regrowth, I sat down, had a snack and a drink. I let the GPS find my location and it was what I expected: I hadn't made any distance. I only was halfway. I rolled my eyes "Welcome on Te Araroa Trail!", grabbed Stinky and bush bashed on. My legs got bruised and scratches started to bleed while I fought through the trees. I pulled my feet out of mud holes that swallowed my legs almost to the knees, and suddenly popped out into the light. I took a deep breath. "Well, that was not too bad." I told myself just before meeting my almost forgotten friend "Gorse Bush". To my disgust, one gorse bush had invited some friends to join for a gorse bush party on the track and I was invited too.

I ripped Stinky and my shirt on my way through the prickly bushes, walked through a really lovely open forest, with beautiful big trees, got lost here and there without the trail markers, and from all the yucky things I had encountered so far, there was only one thing missing: Cows!

I caught the attention of a young, curious cowherd that came running towards me. I ran off, they ran after me and the stampede pushed me into a dip full of burned gorse bushes. Awesome!

I had learned and accepted bashing through green living gorse, but that was crossing the line. I climbed back up, telling myself the cows would be friendly cows and looked for a trail marker. I found it sitting on a wooden post, just on the other side of the burned gorse bush dip.

"That is a joke!" I cursed and stamped through cow shit around it.

Four hours later from the Otira Flood Track sign I found a suitable tent site by Morrison's Footbridge. The sky was overcast, and it drizzled.

I pitched my tent under a vicious attack of hundreds of hungry sandflies, and once in the sandfly-free zone investigated the scratches and bruises on my body. But wait, there was more. To make the day complete I had to run after a Weka that took off with one of my tramping boots.

I climbed back into my tent and found the inside covered with sandflies. I squeezed and killed every single one of them.

"That will teach you, you bastards!"

May I introduce Ms. Sandfly. Together with millions of other sandflies she works for the fun police department (FPD)

The DOC staff in Locke Stream Hut hadn't mentioned a word about the conditions of Otira Flood Track but they had told me about my next section up the Deception River, over Goat Pass and down the Mingha Valley. This section is part of the famous Coast to Coast Run which is a two-day multi part event of running, cycling and kayaking from Kumara on the West Coast to Christchurch on the East Coast. A challenging race for every sporty and competitive Kiwi. Just in January, a woman and her friends trained for the race, but they had picked a bad date and didn't check the weather forecast. It had rained before and Deception River was in flood. The group got washed away when trying to ford it. Everyone, except for this woman, could rescue themselves but she drowned.

With this information on my mind I woke up the next day. It was cold, and the valley was covered in clouds. Long story short: It was depressing!

I packed my stuff and set out on my mission up the Deception. What started as a pleasant walk along the river ended with the first river crossing. Again, it was not a track but a route, again it was "pick your own way." It started to drizzle again. I forded the first time when the river was knee deep, walked further up, following men made stone cairns. I forded the second time when the river flow was stronger, followed the cairns and started to boulder climb and hop along the Deception. I crossed the river for the third time with water up to my hips. The drizzle and grey sky had settled again and with the next crossing point I felt my tummy rumbling and grumbling and nervousness paid its toll; out came the shovel and the toilet paper.

My thoughts drifted back to the footbridge, that led into civilisation.

I thought about a bed, four walls, a roof, a shower and internet, I just wanted to be in safety. After what had happened on the Taramakau the day before I surely had learned a lesson. "You shouldn't be here, not by yourself." I thought, and it was time for me to turn around. It just didn't feel like it was the right thing to do. I back tracked and crossed the river again, and with every step back to the bridge my heart got lighter and happier.

Once in Arthur's Pass the "skipping-pussy-effect" kicked in. I was disappointed and angry with myself that I had turned around and not completed this part. I would wait for tomorrow and hitch back to try and do it again. Then the rain started, it poured down for hours.

I was cosy, safe and sound in the hostel. Instead of walking, I wrote a poem:

Here I am in the distance,
left all my loved ones behind
started Te Araroa at Cape Reinga
and always have Bluff on my mind.

My feet they hurt, my legs complain.
You ask me: "Where is the joy in having pain?"
Well, after cheering on the mountain's top
I've learned:
a hike is honest, and a rest well earned.
I tell you friend, the places I've been
are far the best I've ever seen.

The people I meet, are people like me,
are believers and dreamers,
who seem to walk on a cloud.
We are courageous and grateful and proud.
Together we face ups and downs
and always can rely.
We stand side by side, and give a hand –
things that you can't buy.

So, I'm climbing up the silent hills,
wandering through forests, too.
Over mountains, meadows, streams,
nothing else I'd rather want to do.
And when walking, I'm thinking of what counts.
It's not Dollars, Euros, Pounds.
All what matters is freedom, peace and friends.
And this is how my poem ends.

The rain didn't stop the next morning, it only got lighter and I decided to let Deception-Mingha go.

It was not meant to be and really: If your guts tell you that something is not the right thing to do, you might as well listen to your instincts!

In my opinion, there is nothing wrong with skipping a section on a long-distance trail. It should be a pleasant and enjoyable time and you shouldn't get killed just because you think that you can't claim your adventure to be "perfectly completed." Same for all the road walks on the TA, if you don't want to do it, then don't. Try it, but don't force yourself. It's your choice and it is about the journey, not about the adrenalin or fame!

I prepared for the next trail section to Lake Coleridge instead. I hitched to Greymouth on the West Coast and resupplied there, as Arthur's Pass only has a cafe with a little store to purchase expensive trail food.

Loaded with trail goodies I made my way back to Arthur's Pass and got a lift from a guy, who told me as soon as I sat in his car, that hitchhiking on the West Coast was dangerous, that two female tourists had disappeared a few years ago while getting a lift. "There are a lot of nutters out there, not everyone who looks friendly IS friendly. You got to listen to your gut feelings." I hadn't known the story about the girls when I hitched along the West Coast to catch up with my Trail Family in Wanaka. And if I had known about it, I wouldn't have had much choice back then.

But here wo go: "LISTEN TO YOUR INSTINCTS!"

He dropped me off in the middle of nowhere and I was beached. Minutes passed, cars drove by and no one seemed to want to pick up a girl on the side of the road. Maybe there are stories out there about hitchhikers, that suddenly pulled a knife and killed their patrons, too...

A white truck came along, the brakes squeaked, and an Indian guy rolled down the window, "Want lift?" he asked with a strong Indian accent. "Yes, to Arthur's Pass." I replied as loud and underlined as I could to hopefully make him understand. He only spoke little English and we ended up in a one-two-three-word-sentences-conversation.

He was a young chap and from what I understood he had been in New Zealand for almost seven years, had a wife and would become a dad soon. "That is good!" I always replied to make it easy.

He swapped the topic to religion. Yay, that was my most favourite one. After politics or here, in New Zealand, pest-poisoning with 1080, religion is probably one of the riskiest topics one could have in a conversation with a stranger. "You religious?" He asked me.

"Oh dear." I thought, I am not the right person to ask whether I was religious or not. I am not anti-anti, each to their own. If people decide to believe in a god and follow a certain religion I accept it. As long as they let other people live their lives the way they want, too. To make it easy and to escape an argument with him I just said "Yes" which made him happy and he asked me "Like music?"

"Yes" I replied again, and he turned the music on. With loud Indian Bollywood music and him happily singing and almost dancing along to it, I sat in the car, smiled insecurely at him from time to time and hoped that in all his party mood he wouldn't forget to stop in Arthur's Pass.

"You like?" he asked. "Yeees" I frantically nodded my head. He smiled and carried on partying.

I was positively surprised when he reliably stopped in Arthur's Pass to drop me off. He wished me "Happy Life" I wished him "All the best for your family", shut the door and off he was.

In the meantime, Davorin and Gareth had caught up to me as well as the likes of bubbly Canadian Logan, American Logan and a few other TA hikers as well.

We had a quick get-to-know-each-other but with the conversation progressing I started to feel overwhelmed by all those new faces and disappeared to bed after I had finished packing and preparing Stinky.

Kingdom of Erewhon

It was the 26th of February when I walked out of Arthur's Pass towards Cora Lynn Road and the next wilderness section of my journey.

The Crew would have almost reached their final destination by that time and only had three more days until they would finish Te Araroa Trail in Bluff. Their adventure was almost over now, whereas I still had so many kilometers ahead of me.

I felt melancholic and almost sad for them; tried to imagine how it would be, facing the finish line and knowing that the journey was over. The TA had become my job, my hobby, my escape, my life. I was not ready for it to finish and pushed those thoughts away.

On my way down the highway I met another three TA hikers, and at the car park to Cass-Lagoon Circuit, another three girls, who were doing the loop. A Kiwi, an American and a German. They were students in Christchurch and the German one did a semester in New Zealand as an exchange student.

"Where is home in Germany?" I asked her.

"Pforzheim" she said with a familiar accent.

Pforzheim is only about 30 minutes away from my little hometown. Funny that!

With all those people on the track I treasured my solitude even more.

I never felt more antisocial before and by pitching my tent I avoided the masses. The track was easy, river crossings were straight forward, and everything well marked until the last major river crossing, that was when I hit farmland again. I was following the poles until they suddenly stopped.

I checked my GPS and followed the blue line, marking the TA on the map, but didn't encounter any markers in real life. Again, I played the most popular game one can play on Te Araroa Trail "Trail Marker Marco Polo" "Come out, come out, where ever you are!"

I lost the game, didn't win and didn't succeed. I surrendered!

In the heat of the day I gorse-bush-bashed through a swampy area that was an ankle rolling threat, stumbled through old cow poop patties, sheep droppings and little creeks until I hit a fence, climbed over it and ended up on a farm road and eventually was back on the trail. Take that TA!!

The farm road led all the way to a little campground by a stand of pine trees.

It would be a day of road walking into Lake Coleridge tomorrow.

American Logan turned up and we chatted, he planned on walking to Coleridge in the night to avoid the heat and thought of crossing Rakaia River on the same day.

Rakaia River is a natural border designated by the Te Araroa Trust, to avoid making thru-hikers feel they had to cross it as part of the purism (to walk every little step of a trail) and avoid the many deaths, that this would probably cause.

Logan was confident enough to give it a go. I did like the idea of night walking. I didn't like the idea of crossing the river.

American Logan left by 3am, I heard him pack and leave and then started packing myself. It was beautiful to hike in the night, it was colder, and the air felt fresh and clear, it was almost a full moon and just enough light to see the gravel road ahead, as well as the dark contours of the mountains around me. "Lucky, the moon shines." I thought. "It would have been dark without it." The truth about stars is, that half of the sky doesn't glow.

With the sunrise the country awoke and with that the heat of the day.

I passed Lake Selfe that by many TA hikers is considered to be "Lake Selfie", a popular spot to take a "selfie" of you and the lake. If you didn't take a picture you would have to go back there and take one!

Tadaah!

It was early noon when a TA hiker popped out onto the road ahead of me. I couldn't avoid catching up to Ben from Germany.

I pretended to be too hot already, stopped at the nearest lake, had a cooling swim and washed my clothes, but that also gave him time to race ahead. Go Ben, Go!

On the road I gratefully refused offers for a lift into the village. It was a Sunday afternoon and a popular area for city people, who wanted to escape Christchurch, and soon that fact was going to be my lucky score.

The track left the road, turned off onto farmland with a big sign that said: "Stay on the marked route, trespassers will be prosecuted!"

"Welcome to Lake Coleridge!" I replied. Those guys really knew how to make Te Araroa hikers feel welcome. Instead of following an easy four-wheel drive track, they made one walk on a tiny and deep path, probably sheep made, that went over every little hill. The best moment was, when again a sign warned hikers 'to only stick to the track', which then led into a five-meter-long swamp with mud holes that reached knee depth, instead of taking the little farm road around it.

I bet somewhere on a wooden post the locals had installed secret cameras to watch TA hikers struggling through that swamp, falling into the mud and injuring their bodies. I could see them having community meetings and sitting in a TV room somewhere in Coleridge, watching the weekly recordings of desperate, almost dying hikers, with a bowl of chips and a beer each, laughing their asses off and one saying: "Only a dead TA hiker is a good TA hiker!"

In fact, these four to six kilometers took ages to do but still I was able to admire the beauty of the country, while stumbling along on the little, mean sheep track. Once in Lake Coleridge Village I tried to hitch for almost one and a half hours until eventually a woman picked me up and took me to her family's weekend bach. They were just packing to go back into Christchurch and she offered me a shower and freshly picked blackberries to eat, while waiting for them. I couldn't reject that offer and it partly changed my opinion about the Colerdigers.

The family dropped me off on the main street in Methven and continued down to Christchurch. At the I-site I booked the school bus shuttle to get to the next trail head in the morning. I booked in a hostel, sorted my washing, did my shopping, got myself a ridiculously massive takeaway meal for dinner and eventually checked my phone for messages. It was the 28th of February at 7pm. The Crew had finished Te Araroa Trail.

Tribute to the Crew

It was strange and quite sad to know that Alba, René and Rick were not ahead of me anymore. I texted them, told them how proud I was and what an achievement it was to finish the trail, also to have perfectly kept to their schedule, and to top my fake cheering I asked the silly question: "How does it feel?" René's reply was short and simple: "Don't know yet. Txt later." Stupid me, what did I think it would feel like?!

I felt terribly unmotivated and almost depressed the next morning. The TA felt different now, knowing that three awesome people had left it.
What would it be like to get up in the morning and suddenly to not pack your belongings into your backpack and to not walk in the bush, but sit in the office again; at a desk, in office clothes rather than wearing your familiar tramping clothes and how would it be wearing dry shoes instead of wet ones? On top of my self-inflicted little depression I had to get up at 4am to catch the school bus that brought me and other hikers beyond Glenrock Station, on the other side of the Rakaia River.
It was dark and cold and even though I had walked in the night by choice already, I now got reset into my working or study days, leaving the house in the dark winter mornings and not being keen on a day at work or

school. I had to fight the memories off and shake those thoughts away. Never again I wanted to work almost 10-hour shifts, three times a week.

Rakaia River is massive, it has a several kilometers wide river bed full of gravel and the river splits in several deep streams, that join up to pass a narrow gorge and beyond that, widen again to eventually end up in the Pacific Ocean, south of Christchurch. It is one of the largest braided rivers in New Zealand.

The water of the Rakaia is turquoise, and now it added to a beautiful landscape as we, in the dawn of the day, slowly made our way on a gravel road out to the trail head. Davorin had joined somewhere on the drive. It was great to have him as a relaxed and peaceful part, whereas the others in the bus were young, and some of the already mentioned type "Superhikers."

The driver dropped us off, it was a crisp morning, cloudy, and this day for me was a little herald of colder mornings on my journey.

The others walked ahead, and Davorin and I walked together for a while, to eventually part. I climbed a big continuous and gradual zigzagging farm road up to the top of a saddle, had breakfast there while hiding behind a rock and looked over the Rakaia Valley. That gave Davorin the chance to take his beloved landscape pictures without any human being in it.

He was the type of guy that enjoyed his solitude, too.

I met him again in the first hut, an A-frame shape type building. Everyone else had continued on, to the next hut or even further, never to be seen again. I opened the hut book to read American Logan's entry and raised an eyebrow in disbelief: "Crossed Rakaia River!" Crazy guy!

Davorin and I talked about the next major river ahead, Rangitata that again is a designated hazard zone, a natural break, like the Cook Strait between North Island and South Island or like Rakaia River. Again, it is not a part of the TA. We figured it would be a pain to go all the way around Rangitata; it was about 160 kilometers by car around it and parts of that were so remote, we would struggle to get a lift. Therefore, we agreed to meet before the river, stay there the night, and then we would try to cross it together in the morning, if the conditions were right, which was most likely as it hadn't been raining for days.

Davorin carried on to Comyns Hut. We would meet up in two days-time.

Already cosy in the A-Frame, lazy me took the chance for a hut night by myself. I hadn't slept well last night, the early get up and the climb were tiring and so I stayed, wrapped in my sleeping bag, tried to get warm and had a nap. I knew I had to walk a fair mileage the next day to meet up with Davorin again, also I felt un-TA-hiker-like doing these mini days.

So, I climbed out of my sleeping bag in the morning and gobbled my breakfast. It was freezing cold outside and the cool air almost hit me in the face, when I stepped out of the hut.

The A-frame

I marched on to keep me warm and sped past Comyns Hut, followed an easy and fun "pick your own track" river route up to a saddle, where I then caught up with Davorin, who also had had the hut to himself, as the "Superhikers" apparently carried on all the way to Manuka Hut yesterday. That would be as far as we would walk today.

The descend from the saddle into the plains was a mix of slipping, tumbling, stumbling and a few falls. The tussock plants just made every step a little bit slippery. I paid the price with a reminder from someone that I had almost forgotten about: "Robert", my ankle pain, briefly yelled out to me again.

Just before finding the most stunning campsite on the flats before Manuka Hut, I got spoiled for choice in the Te Araroa way: Either I would walk through prickly bushes or I would walk through human size grown

Spaniard Grass, which was sharp as a razor blade and could easily slice your legs in halves (Note author is definitely overexaggerating here).
I took the prickly bushes!

The next day funnily enough turned out to be the hottest day ever.
The land almost looked like a "No-Man's-Land" with a "Lost World" character, with surreal flats surrounded by lonely mountains and hanging valleys. I figure that it almost was the same as the Motatapus between Wanaka and Queenstown. Once, they were covered with native forest, and then burned down by humans, now mostly covered with tussock.
It didn't surprise me to read in the trail notes that some guy back in the days had called it "Erewhon". It is the name of a novel by Samuel Butler, in which the protagonist discovers the wop-wop country "Erewhon." A term that sounds like out of the Lord of the Rings.
I guess one could really read it backwards and call it "Nowhere."
I followed poles, desperately looking for a water source, found a little stream after a while, filled all the bottles I had and carried on. I had to cover my head and face like the Bedouins do, to protect my skin from the sun.
In the absence of my attention I lost the track and followed markers for three kilometers in the wrong direction which, once I had backtracked them, added almost another hour to my already long day.
Unexpectedly, in the middle of "Erewhon" there were two four-wheel drives coming my way. One rolled down the window and a woman, obviously super worried asked me: "What are you doing out here all by yourself, girl? Are you lost??"
"Nope, I just took the wrong track!" I replied, and she handed me four muesli bars to keep me going. Cool!

It was late in the evening when I found Davorin and the camp spot by Potts River. Slightly dehydrated I pitched the tent, we had dinner and each crawled in our tents to get some rest before the fording of Rangitata River the next day.
I woke early to a soaking wet sleeping bag, for whatever reason the condensation in the night was so strong and made the water drops run down the inside of my tent. Downy, my sleeping bag, obviously had been dehydrated as well and had turned into a sponge to suck up the water.
As Davorin was already up, we quickly ate, packed and carried on. He carried a proper GPS device that even spoke to him. In the mornings he

would enter his destination and a (after a while able to be parroted) female voice told him. "You have 24 kilometers to go."

"You have 22 kilometers to go" - I found that slightly dis-encouraging. But this trip showed when accurate proper GPS devices come in handy. He had the latest satellite images of the Rangitata and we could see the best spots where to try and cross the river. We walked upstream, and with every little side stream we passed, we knew we didn't need to cross those anymore.

Mum, sorry, I know, I swore to never do silly things ever again, but here I was setting my foot in a five-kilometer-wide river bed.

I told Davorin about my almost misadventure on the Taramakau and that I felt nervous about Rangitata. He encouraged me in every step, and to distract me, he talked about his hiking trips with his son, his life in Croatia and his passion for photography.

The Rangitata and "Erewhon" are quite popular for tourists. People drive all the way into the wop-wops for only one single, but famous mountain. "Mount Sunday", standing out like a little pimple by the river, served as another Lord of the Rings film location. Up on the mountain the film crew had created the village of Edoras, where Rohan's King Theoden reigned. So, if you ever see crazy amounts of camper vans in the backcountry of New Zealand, think of The Lord of the Rings. And if you ever see filthy looking people with backpacks and trekking poles, seemingly lost and confused, then remind yourself that "Not all those who wander are lost!"

Lost? We? Never!

We crossed the first "proper" water, a hip deep pool with soft ground. During the whole river bed crossing both, Davorin and I, mentally prepared ourselves for the big main river channel to come, we crossed plenty of little streams that were ankle and less than knee deep, after each we wanted to cheer but stopped ourselves to not praise it before we could physically touch the other side across Rangitata. You never know on the TA!

"You have 15 kilometers to go."

Our expected deep main river channel never came and suddenly we popped out on the other side, gave each other a confused look and shrugged it off.

We had conquered the 'beast' and carried on to Mesopotamia Station and the "Two Thumb Track."

Davorin on the way to Mesopotamia Station

By the time we had our lunch break, one of my shoes that I had attached to the outside of Stinky had come off in a wind gust; unnoticed by both, Davorin and I. I backtracked two kilometers to eventually find the stray lying on the track, crying for his Mama.

I gave the little shoe a hug and reunited we returned to Stinky and Davorin, who only shook his head in disbelief of how emotional attached to a shoe a human could be. I carried that damn thing for more than 2000 kilometers, Davorin. It was like a body part to me!

Surprisingly Gareth caught up to us as we were making our way up Bush Stream. Gareth had skipped the sections from Arthur's Pass to the Two Thumb Track; he had had several meetings for his fundraising to attend in Christchurch, as well as had caught up with friends on the way.
Davorin, Gareth and I followed the stream, crossed a gazillion times, some crossings tricky, some less and eventually we began the hard climb up to Crooked Spur Hut.
"You have reached your destination." Davorin's GPS friend let us know.

Also, in Crooked Spur were two German boys on a section hike of the TA. From a "Superhiker" they had learned to only have nuts as food which eventually made up for the worst dinner I had ever seen on the TA: "Cooked nut mix." I value the health benefits of nuts, but that took it one step too far.... but hey..."Enjoy!"

We all left early the next day. I rescued the German boys on the way as instead of the track, they had followed a stream into a gully, wondering why there were no trail markers anymore. To be fair, spotting trail markers in the tussock country is not easy as the yellow coloured tussock grows tall and just swallows the orange colour of the markers. So, the two followed me until they could see one of the poles themselves again.
It was Gareth's birthday today. The boy had carried Vodka in his water bladder to celebrate his special day in the wild, therefore at Stone Hut, our lunch break hut, he mixed a bit of strawberry flavour in the Vodka and offered us drinks. I didn't drink it. Davorin loved it.
Apart from that, Gareth was the one to stick to, not only carried he Vodka, he also carried kilos of sweets that he loved to offer to people.
I don't know what it is, but for whatever reason you often crave for the food of other people rather than for what you carry (Except for cooked nut dishes, of course!). The grass is always greener...you know what I'm trying to say...!

Later we all met again in Royal Hut, that got its name apparently from the British Royals, the Windsor Family. Prince Charles had spent some time there when he was a young boy. There was nothing fancy about it though. It really is just a normal basic DOC Backcountry Hut. Still it was a good day to be there; we had two women on horses staying with us and birthday boy Gareth had the chance to help a team of researchers with attaching their gear to a helicopter.

Only two more days it would take me to get to Lake Tekapo and I was the first to climb over the highest point on Te Araroa Trail, Stag Saddle, where a little sign post marks the 1925m altitude. From up there I could see Lake Tekapo in the distance. It was a good day to be on the mountain tops, so I carried on to an optional route over a ridge. Again, it was so worth the sweat, from high up there you could look onto the lake as well as another mountain range and I was lucky enough to spot the mighty Mount Cook.

Adventure still found me on that day; once I had descended from the ridge, walked to little rustic Camp Stream Hut and chatted to some Eastern European boys, who were out on an adventure themselves, I got lost again. I only missed one marker that told people to climb up a little ridge line ABOVE the river, instead I followed an animal path DOWN the river. For me it was obvious it was a proper track; it cut through bushes perfectly well to be mistaken as one. DOC's animal staff sometimes did better work than the human staff (referring to the Otira Flood Track).

But then the path slowly disappeared after a few kilometers further down. As it would have been typical Te Araroa Trail, I cursed at the bad track maintenance. I crawled over low dense scrubs, bashed through gorse and crossed the river a hundred times, and then finally came to the conclusion that I had gotten lost and if, then it would take me double the time to backtrack.

Only now, I don't know why, I checked my GPS location. As expected I was off track! I stood in the river valley and the trail was up on the ridge.

I saw a road bridge on the map that I could try to reach, but as the last kilometers had taken me already two hours, I didn't want to imagine how long that would take me to walk down to the bridge. Alternatively, the valley banks, I was surrounded by, looked smooth in the beginning but steepened in the end and it would be a hard climb up to reach the trail. "Either or, I would sweat." I figured, filled up the water bottles and decided to climb.

It was lovely, as long as I had grip on the ground, but once the scree part started it turned into a full body workout. With one step up, I sled three steps down, first on bigger rocks then on little pebbles. I held on to anything that looked anchored to the ground to push and pull me up. Watch a sweaty, dusty and dirty hiker crawl onto Tekapo's Skifield Road.

I sat and looked down to the river, trying to figure out how many hundreds of meters I had climbed in less than 20 minutes. I was buggered, and it was late but at least Skifield Road would connect with the TA in two kilometers.

Just before joining up with the trail I found a beautiful campsite, overlooking Lake Tekapo, and made it the end of the day.

Tekapo is called "the Sanctuary of Stars" and indeed it was from up there. After a beautiful sunset, the starry sky was one of the best I had seen on the entire TA.

It was an easy walk into Lake Tekapo Village now. A walk in the heat through tussock and a gravel road eventually brought me into 'Tourist Town'. I passed the famous "Church of the Good Shepherd" by the lake front, watched hundreds of Asians, all taking the same picture and ended up in Tekapo's little supermarket to buy and over spoil myself with the long-craved carrots and a tin of tuna.

Gareth had just gotten himself beers and takeaways, offered me a cool beer and we quickly chatted about the last track. He had missed the turn off to the ridge past Stag Saddle and had had his own little adventure in the tussock.

I quickly resupplied, booked into the hostel at the local campground, sorted all my stuff and cleaned the smelly body to eventually have takeaways back in town, and under compulsion, shared it with 15 aggressive seagulls around me.

This town stay was rather stressful. If I had to decide again, whether to stay in Tekapo or whether to carry on, I would carry on. After so many days in almost solitude and only one or two people to be seen a day, a town full of Asian bus tourists, and a hostel full of young people was just too hard to handle. My tolerance for society and towns slowly started to decrease. I had to watch out for cars, for humans, for rules and instead of hearing the trees rustling in the wind is was human chatter. Therefore, I decided to pull a Zero Day in the next town, Twizel, which was two to three days of gravel road walking away. Some TA hikers didn't like that idea and rented bikes to cover that stretch, some hitched, some walked.

I walked and enjoyed being on a road with bridges and for a change to not having to think about getting lost on a track.

Lake Pukaki offered me a lovely campsite under a stand of trees, with my own personal beach and a Mt. Cook Lookout. It was a temptress of a lake and the next day I only walked for two hours, found another beautiful campsite close to the shore, had several swims during the day as well as some naps and edited my journal.

Trail Journal entry for Tuesday 8.3.16, Day 150

Slooooooooooooow start.
Sloooooooow walking.
Breeeaaaaaaak.
Walked one more kilometer and pitched the tent.
What an amazing spot on the shore. WOOOOOHOOOOOOO!
Swimsies, naps and food.
NERODAY!

I remembered American Logan's idea of night walking to escape the sun, if there was no shade around to hide from the afternoon heat, and packed my stuff around 2am in the night to get another night hike in. It was almost as magic as my first walk in the dark. In a break, I sat, wrapped in my sleeping bag, on the lake shore and watched the sun rise, shining the light on the mountains across the lake, and then, followed the A2O, Alps to Ocean Cycle Trail, past busy campsites full of campervans and over endless dry, brown coloured, bold flats into Twizel.

Twizel was a positive surprise to Tekapo. It was less busy and people still friendly, it was a good town for a Zero Day.

As usual I would have a sleep in, would hang around in the hostel's lounge to catch up with social media and news from around the world, but with my increasing intolerance for society, my tolerance for worldly news had decreased as well. I just couldn't bother about it anymore, quickly read over the headlines online, shrugged it off and carried on planning my life, instead of focusing on what bad things had happened again or who of the "VIPs" again had cheated on their partners. The trail had become my ignorance bubble, a peaceful place, that separated me from the world, and ignorance was bliss.

No! No! No!

I resupplied in Twizel, checked out in the morning and slowly followed Davorin, who had left early as well. We both must have had cravings for bananas as I carried three and Davorin carried two.

On the road to Lake Ohau I caught up with American Logan, he had done a few side trips to Mt Cook and was back to now finishing the trail. We chatted about his river crossing of the Rakaia and he admitted that it had been tricky and a good decision of the TA Trust to make it a natural border for the trail. Then he smiled and said: "But, you know, every river is like an armour and every armour has a weak spot. You just gotta find it!"
Funny how the simplest things that people say can leave a big impression in us.

I followed his advice a few days later, when I crossed Ahuriri River, the last major river on the TA. René had told me already to cross above its rapids and with American Logan's advice I felt prepared and didn't worry too much about the crossing.
I walked towards Ahuriri, on flats that looked burned from the sun, stumbled over gazillions of rabbit holes, "they must have bunny issues here" I mumbled to myself, and then eventually stood on the bank before dropping down to the river.
As we hadn't had any rain for days again, Ahuriri crossing was simple and straight forward, the spot where to cross easy to identify and I was on the other side of it in no time. I climbed up the banks and carried on, had a bite to eat by a deer paddock with a beautiful stag in it, got up, grabbed Stinky, twisted my back and the pain shot into my right hip, making every step painful. The pain radiated into my lower back and pelvis, it was almost as if I couldn't put any weight on the right leg anymore and I limped like an old woman who suffered from severe hip arthritis.
I dragged myself up Martha Saddle, where an old farm road leads all the way up and across. I descended into the valley and passed so many beautiful camp spots which would have been me, but in that pain, I didn't even think of trying to pitch the tent and sleeping in it. I wanted a hut.
It took me ages to get to Top Timaru Hut. I had to sit down every 500 meters to ease the pain, hoping it would be gone the next time I would get up, but it was still there.

By the time I reached Top Timaru I almost was in tears.

What had happened, what did I do wrong? Why couldn't I turn back the time and re-do this moment by the paddock?

Every move I made was painful. Bending forwards, taking off my shoes, sitting and eventually lying, everything was uncomfortable. I was back on pain killers for dinner, as night snack and in the morning for breakfast.

I desperately tried to stretch my muscles, tried to mobilise my back and hips but nothing seemed to help. Still I had to walk that day. There was rain in the forecast and the last thing I needed, was getting stuck in a hut far off the grid.

I didn't see the beauty of the nature and majestic landscapes anymore, all I did was focusing on my pain and the worst river sidle with ups and downs and slippery river crossings, and if it wasn't already bad enough in that situation, the last climb up to old and very basic Stodys Hut, was a straight climb, out of the river bed, up the ridge! There was no break in the climb, no zigzagging, no flats to breath for a while, no mercy. It really took you straight, more than a thousand meters, up. It was challenging and finally I broke. I sat down and cried. In tears I got to Stodys, unpacked my stuff and installed myself.

Davorin popped in, in the afternoon, and stayed with me the night. He felt sorry for me, told me to just have a rest somewhere, once in Hawea or Wanaka and in reply to my fear of maybe not being able to finish the last 460km of the trail, he just gave me a hug.

The morning when he left was the last time that I saw him.

I stayed in Stodys for a rest and spent the whole day wrapped in my sleeping bag. It was freezing cold outside and it rained. Anyway, I didn't have a reason to get up for. Again, months after the "Robert incident" I faced the picture of not finishing Te Araroa Trail due to an injury. I drugged myself up the next morning, just wanted to be out of the bush and the mountains. I wanted a warm bed, WiFi, civilisation, proper food and a reachable accessible toilet, not one that was 50 meters away.

The weather was still drizzly, and a low cloud hung over the hills, while I made my way to Pakituhi Hut for a quick rest. Two day-trampers had just finished their lunch and two DOC workers arrived in their car. I was too shy to ask for help, and to maybe get a lift out into Hawea, so I didn't say a word, finished my food and swallowed my pain killers and left.

Either it was the drugs or a survival instinct that kept me going.

As hard as it had been to climb up that hill, as hard it was to go it down again. Steep drops between little flats and a rugged rock scramble led me towards an insane 400 meters-dropping-zigzag track.

Once at the bottom my legs were physically clueless to walk on the flats again, they just wanted to carry on walking downhill. I hit the gravel road into Hawea, waddled along the lake, had to break up the walk with several rests to manage the pain and eventually got into the village. Hawea only has a little campground, a hostel and bar as well as a small grocery store and Takeaway. But now, Hawea also meant cell phone coverage, bed, toilets just across the floor, a shower and rest for the wicked. I ordered a big portion of chips as well as a fizzy drink for early dinner. The pain exhausted me more and more and I tried to make up for it with food. I asked around for a physio in town and got the last appointment of the day, to get the muscles released before having a proper rest.

Even after a Zero Day in Hawea the pain remained the same, still I had to move on, towards Wanaka, where I could find a cheaper place to stay and more flexibility in terms of grocery shopping. I tried to walk on the well-formed track along a river into Albert Town but after only a few kilometers in I realised that it was not enjoyable to walk, and eventually got a lift into Wanaka itself. From there I scored the last bed in a hostel, met two lovely German girls, Jasmin and Eli, on their New Zealand trip and actually enjoyed the time and chats we had, even though they were Germans.

Still, I hated the hostel, it set me back to the one I had stayed in Nelson; too many young people, too many people that didn't share the same experiences. The only difference to Nelson was that there was no Jocelyn and no B'n'B to hide away.

In the morning I quickly shifted to Wanaka's Holiday Park and pitched the tent to at least have my own private space. I booked in at a physio's, and the treatment felt relieving, she poked dry needles in my butt and told me that, either "people would love it or hate it". Obviously, my body disliked it. Once the needle poked my glutes my whole right leg went into spasms with burning pain and it felt bruised for days after. Later, I did walk or limp the section from Albert Town to Wanaka without a heavy pack. It was sore, not pleasant, but doable.

Nathalie, the Belgian TA hiker, happened to be in Wanaka the same day. She had met up with her partner and was just taking time off-trail. We had ice cream and a very long chat about the TA journey and she encouraged me to just take it easy the next days, and maybe find another physio as well as a chiropractor. It was good catching up with her especially now that I didn't have my Kiwis around. In fact, I didn't know anybody to talk to in person that would really understand how my situation was. The only ones I kept steady contact with were Maud, sometimes Rick and also René, who had been back at work in the DOC office in Wellington, only one day after finishing the TA.

The next days I was just desperate for someone to help me. It was only less than 500 kilometers to Bluff, and I couldn't believe that there was no one to fix the pain. I suddenly had become like one of the clients that I used to see, visiting health professionals and expecting them to do the quick fix for something that just needed time. As the physio's treatments felt good but never made a difference, I decided to see a chiropractor instead. In Wanaka the bone clickers never seemed to be open, so I had to shift to Queenstown. I already was off-trail for about five days and missed the silence and serenity I had experienced, I needed to go back to finish my journey come what may!

As most of the time, the generosity and hospitality of people was mind blowing; I got a lift over the famous Cardrona road by a woman that drove me all the way into the center of Queenstown, even though she didn't need to.
It felt like walking against a wall in this buzzing city. There were too many traffic lights and way too many people and cars. It started to bucket down with heavy, big rain drops and I had nowhere to stay in this expensive place. Then I received two messages; the first was from my Te Araroa aunties Sarah, Marlies and Sandie, who would be arriving in Queenstown the next evening. The second was from René, who had booked and paid a hostel for two nights for me. A friend in need is a friend indeed!

I caught up with my trail aunties the next evening after I had visited the chiropractor without any changing result. It was a lovely evening; I listened to their stories of how they had become section hikers to give Sarah, who lives in San Francisco, the chance to experience as much of New Zealand's wilderness as possible and still be part of the team, even though her knee was not the best anymore.
They dropped me off at my hostel, we hugged and said goodbye. Shortly after, my phone rang. It was Maud: "Darling, come to Te Anau and stay with us, Luca is here, too." I followed her invite and hitched to Te Anau.
Luca had finished the TA and was already on his last adventure on the South Island, a 10-day Dusky Sound tramp, in Fjordland. For that he left, after staying five days with us. As always it was a pleasure to spend time with Maud and Guillaume.

They had found work in Te Anau and were earning money. Those two people, strangers in the beginning when I met them, had over time really become my closest friends. Like in Nelson already, those were the people I needed now, again. They knew me, they had experienced the TA and the life on a long-distance trail and were there when I needed someone the most.

I had rested for about 13 days already and still the pain, or how I called it, "Fritz-Heinrich", accompanied me. I had nights where I couldn't fall asleep, overthinking my journey, contemplating whether it was actually still my dream, to finish the trail, or whether I should just accept the fact and end it here in Te Anau.

I had nights when my motivation, energy and patience were that low, I could have easily stopped walking.

And then sometimes, I would find motivation again and the stubborn side of me took over, it would tell me that I would not just give up, so close to Bluff, and it advised me to: "Just walk and do it." I had come to New Zealand to walk Te Araroa Trail, I had started it and now I "would finish the god damn thing!" I forced into my brain. I never had started things without not finishing them! Bad weeds grow tall!

Someone had said "Never stop a trail on a bad day. Stop it only on a good day with sunshine." Who was I to talk about ending the TA in a state like that? I had no right. I had to wait for the sun to shine to eventually make the final decision.

Therefore, if I wanted to finish the trail, I had to start walking again rather sooner than later. It was already the end of March and the weather would not improve. Autumn was here, and winter would come.

Snail Trail

On the 31st of March, I said goodbye to Maud and Guillaume, hitched back to Queenstown and headed into the stores. It was time for my old worn boots to retire. They had done about 2000km and the soles were finished. Instead of completely saying goodbye, I sent them off, on a journey around the globe; if I came back home after New Zealand, they would be waiting for me in Germany.

In a sports store I got myself a pair of pink trail runners, for TA discount, and hoped they would make a change to "Fritz-Heinrich" my back and hip pain. Afterwards I got myself groceries for the next TA stretch to Te Anau, packed them as I usually would, and was ready and set to go for the next day. I agreed to potentially be in a very bad physical state and would be in pain for the last kilometers to Bluff, but if I wanted to get there, then that obviously was the deal.

From a travelling girl I got a lift to Glenorchy and then into Kinloch, both small places in the hills past Queenstown that had a Scottish flair to them. With low clouds in the hills and Lake Wakatipu beneath, it indeed seemed like in the Highlands of Scotland. Kinloch was the last settlement before reaching the Greenstone carpark where the TA would continue, and I made it my stop for the day. The hostel was nearly empty, and how could I have said "No" to a Hot Tub, on a cold day like it was that day?

Surprisingly both, Fritz-Heinrich and I, enjoyed the soak and I think: secretly he loved the new shoes, too.

A booked shuttle dropped me off at the Greenstone Track trail head in the early morning hours. I only planned on walking to Greenstone Hut that day as I had no idea what Fritz-Heinrich would be up to, and neither how the new trail runners would behave. All in all, "F.H." felt alright, every now and then he would poke the back of my pelvis, but it was bearable after all. I just enjoyed being back on the trail again, having a track under my feet, the sound of a river, curious robins in the trees around me and to just be able to continue my journey.

Greenstone Hut was packed with trampers. It is quite a popular place for people that are doing a combined circuit with the Routeburn Track, one of the nine most popular, bookable Great Walks in New Zealand, or many people actually just want to walk the Greenstone Track itself. To my surprise I was the only TA hiker that evening. After having missed out on another two weeks of walking, many hikers had over taken me and people like Davorin and maybe even Gareth would be finishing the trail very soon.

It rained in the early morning hours. Once the rain stopped, I carried on to the Mavora Walkway and Taipo Hut. It was a stunningly beautiful landscape, this Greenstone area, and so diverse; I passed little swamps and walked through forests to eventually pop out onto the tussocky flats in a wide mountain valley and reached Taipo Hut. I managed to enjoy this little section even though my feet slowly started to rub against the shoes. The shoes wouldn't hopefully be too small?
Once in Taipo Hut I removed the socks, saw the first blister forming on my right heel and told myself that this would be normal with new shoes, especially when switching from boots to trail runners.

The night was super cold but the starry sky sparkly. Nightly toilet visits, as painful as it is to get up in the cold and to leave your warm sleeping bag, are most often so worth it; just for watching the night sky and the stars.
There were ice crystals on flowers in the morning, as well as little muddy patches, that were still covered with thin ice when I walked by to sometimes crush them with my poles for entertainment.
Once I had reached Careys Hut that day, the blister on my right heel had opened and I had a big deep hole where there usually is skin. The rubbing pain had taken over my attention and Fritz-Heinrich got given the background. I tried to dry the wound out overnight, but it didn't work.

Along the lake shore, which again was a film location for the Lord of the Rings, I only managed to reach Mavora DOC Camp, that was 10 kilometers away. I was done!

Trail Journal entry for Tuesday 5.4.16, Day 178

Got new shoes, walked blisters.
What had formed already three days ago has gotten worse.
Right heel, open wound. Pain.
I only made 10 kilometers today, pitched tent at DOC campground by lake.
Still enjoyed the walk along the shore with all the fly agarics and other mushrooms. Pretty.
I slowly lose my courage and the pleasure walking Te Araroa.

My body is tired of walking and tired of the pains. Everything just hurts. The blisters, my back, the hip, my thumbs, neck and my knees.

I am tired of worrying about everything. Super sad.

Lying in tent crying.

Night will be freezing cold.

I can't deal with all the injuries anymore and there is no way I can walk out to Te Anau tomorrow.

It is only 265 kilometers left to Bluff and I am running low in energy and an empty spirit.

Don't want to think about tomorrow. Getting attacked by sandflies when packing the tent, it is going to be cold, the pain, all the limping and filthy bloody socks.

It took me three hours for 10ks today and every step was painful.

The last days were painful, every single one, every step, every minute, every hour. I am tired and exhausted.

I think I have bitten off more than I can chew. Maybe I am not meant to reach Bluff?

I split the walk to State Highway 94 and Te Anau into thirds; the trail snail was reborn! What probably took a healthy TA hiker about one day, took me three. Thank goodness, I had planned and bought enough food for those things to happen. Nobody said it was easy, doing the trail in pain.

Instead of the designated track I took the gravel road the next morning.

I didn't care about sticking to the official trail or taking the easy way on a parallel road anymore. At least there wouldn't be an unexpected, bad surprise waiting for me on the road.

One could definitely tell that the seasons had changed and that I had reached Southland, which is known for plenty of rain, especially now in autumn. I had been on the trail for almost seven months now and it really took its toll. I craved for a place to stay longer than a week. I wished for a wardrobe instead of living out of a pack and I wished for a car to quickly drive down the road and into Te Anau.

In fact, that day, I counted myself lucky, the clouds in the sky brought rain and just before it started to pour down I had found a little bus stop shelter made of tin. It was big enough for a human to lie on the ground, water and storm resistant enough to call it my overnight shelter or "Hobo Tin Hut."

Hobo Tin Hut

I drew a little intentions book on the wall and I was the first to sign in Hobo Tin Hut's intentions book. When the rain hit, I built a door out of my tent's groundsheet, fixed it to the walls with just enough duct tape, and hoped to not to be seen and discovered by locals. I cooked my dinner and installed my "bed" for the night; my tent served as my groundsheet to keep me dry from underneath, my sleeping mat was for me to lie on, I was in my sleeping bag and the emergency blanket, that I had carried all the time, finally got used to cover me and my sleeping bag. In Hobo Tin Hut I had become an outdoor-hobo. I felt like a real stray but a stray that was grateful for this tin shelter in the middle of nowhere, on the side of a road, in the pouring rain. It would keep me dry that night.

We thru-hikers have one wonderful talent: (Besides 'normally' being able to walk for 10 hours and eating as much as we want without getting fat) we are really good in making ourselves comfortable everywhere. What other people would see as a "lousy, yucky place" turns into a four-star hotel for us hikers.

I made it to State Highway 94 the next day and caught a lift into Te Anau. It was done. I had walked it, even though it took me longer than everybody else.

I took another three rest days in town to give the blisters time to heal, ate healthily and kept the weight off my feet. After having had my little burn out by the Mavora Lakes, I now felt more positive about my trail journey.

I had walked it in pain, nothing had gotten better, but neither had it gotten super worse. The next section would be the last proper wilderness section before hitting the Southland coast and for nothing in this world I wanted to miss out on that. It was almost mid-April and even if I would reach Bluff in the beginning of May, what did it matter?! I was too close to give up!

In the late afternoon I hitched out of town, back to the track, and walked along a farm road, among a herd of cows that had to swap their paddock. I tip toed around a lazy bull, that was lying in the mud and watched me suspiciously. I happily and friendly waved at him. He didn't wave back. I still had to work on that cow-municating-thing.

At Lower Princhester Hut, just a few kilometers up the road, I met Otis or "Papa Oats", a funny, sympathetic Amercian guy that had walked the Appalachian Trail to lose weight, then got addicted to trail walking, and now he tested his own self-made lightweight gear, like backpacks and hammocks on Te Araroa Trail. He had gotten is trail name "Papa Oats" on the AT when a female pregnant mouse undetected gave birth to babies in his backpack. Funnily enough, in his way of being, he almost reminded me of a little mouse. In a cute way though.

The difference from trail runners to boots was definitely the grip and stability of the feet on the ground. Especially on muddy downhills I felt just a little insecure after I had tossed my boots. It was a steady uphill from Lower Princhester Hut, leading over a bush covered saddle and then again, dropping down on the other side, and it was a muddy slippery track through this beautiful dense bush with big ferns growing in the undergrowth. In no time my legs were dirty from the mud and my feet soaked from the water. Trail runners let water through quite quickly, but they also dried easier and quicker than tramping boots.

From the forest, the track took hikers over endless tussock with dangerous holes in the ground; whether rabbit holes or little hiding creeks, both were covered from the tussock leaves and some of them might have been waist deep. One would better not accidentally step in them. It surely made up for a slow walking progress. My trekking poles worked wonders there. Before taking the next step, I would poke the ground to see whether there was a hole in front of me. If not: GREAT! If yes: HOW DEEP? Trekking poles are awesome for measuring holes – and mud puddles, of course.

On the way again, there was an animally surprise waiting for the hikers, in form of a massive bull, that suddenly stood in the tussock, to guard over his wild kingdom - It was not the most pleasant thing to pass him, he was a real bull policeman or a doorman with muscles like a body builder and he tried to narrow the path down where we hikers walked. Again, I think that the TA Trust secretly rents misbehaving bulls of farmers to then let them entertain the hikers in case they were bored or in case they had survived the vicious tussock, the sandfly-fun-police, raging rivers or slippery landslips. It was just another insidious obstacle on the way to Bluff.

Just to keep it interesting after the bull, there was the slightly aggressive valley hawk, that DOC had trained up to chase hikers away from a look out point over the flats. They could have admired the nature for too long, DOC couldn't let that happen!

By the end of the day at Aparima Hut I had done 17 kilometers in eight hours, which was about the time the sign had said back at Lower Princhester. I felt proud of myself to have walked such a long day with blisters and "F.H.", who slowly, very slowly felt better than the days before. In fact, even the blisters were bearable, or maybe I had gotten used to them. After that day I was in a good mood and confident. I would make it to Bluff. I would be slow, but I would make it.

Aparima Hut surprisingly was packed with TA hikers, they suddenly, one by one popped in, in the early and late evening. They all knew each other and were a complete opposite to the people I had walked with on the trail. They were about to become "Superhikers." Being the only one they didn't know, they treated me warily, made way for me when I passed them and always apologised for themselves, they even asked me whether I was just a day hiker. I wasn't looking for a group of hikers to be with anymore and I was tired of explaining myself, instead I curled up in my sleeping bag and read a book, I had sneaked from Lower Princhester Hut.

I had grabbed the more or less sophisticated thriller "Lair" about black monster rats that lived in a forest and feasted on human beings.

Nothing beats a terribly shocking high-class story like that when you are sitting in the woods at the time you read it!

I carried the book even further to Lower Wairaki Hut the next day, where I had a lovely open fire, fueled by a German riddle book and wood that I had collected in the afternoon.

The forest and bush on that section was extremely muddy and wet but it also was so diverse and different from each part to the next. From an open forest with big trees to a dense, thick, moss overgrown bush.

Remarkably pretty. The track started off flat and then gradually climbed and steepened to the end. I then got spit out of the woods, onto the tops, via something that looked like a tree tunnel with a light in the end. I stepped into the open and had reached the bold tops of the Takitimu Ranges.

I was fortunate enough to get a view with beautiful blue sky. From here I could see the southern coastline and when I squeezed my eyes, to look in the distance, I could spot my destination. Bluff! Out of around 3000 kilometers I had only about 145 left.

On the Takitimus, pointing out Bluff

On the tops of the Takitimus I was happy to see the coast and at the same time I felt uneasy. During my whole journey I had had so many moments were I had cursed at the track, fought through forests and limped in pain.

I had hated the TA several times, maybe sometimes even at least once a day. But also, I had loved it twice as much and recognised it as my home and life. I had made friends with the trees, the ground, the rivers, the birds, and had fallen in love with the people and New Zealand. And now, the end of Te Araroa Trail was so near, my body so ready to finish but my mind couldn't find anything positive about it. I had not been prepared to finish weeks before and nothing of that had changed! What did that mean at all "to finish Te Araroa Trail?" How could something that I had done for seven months just finish? What would life be like, once the TA got taken away from me? What would I do the morning after reaching Bluff?

Thank goodness, the here and now quickly drew my attention away, from grieving into surprise. Steeply they made hikers descend, towards Telford Campsite, which was nothing new after having walked around 2800 kilometers, one just did it. The only thing that marked the camp, and that was visible from the tops, was the long drop toilet in the middle of grassy flats, surrounded by little dark moving spots. "Don't tell me it is what I think! Surely, they wouldn't let cows onto the campsite!" I stared at the scene in disbelief, as nothing seemed to separate the cows from the campsite. "Ah well, got to go there. Not much choice!" I descended and passed the first cows that were happily munching on their grassy snacks, when suddenly Moo-Moo Nr. 723 noticed this funny looking human being walking by and decided to panic. The fear led to a chain reaction in the remaining cow herd and they all started to panic as well, just in the moment when I was in the middle of the herd. And here was the moment that the TA had prepared me for; after having experienced thousands of cows along the journey, I had grown on the trail and was not afraid of them anymore. I quietly walked with the raging, tumbling masses of bodies, through knee deep mud and cow shit, all the way to Telford Camp. A small electronic fence line set up in a little square was the designated spot to pitch a tent. Great. I pitched my house under observation and suspect of 200 eyes and went to the toilet with the eyes of my four-legged neighbours following me until I shut the door.

The view from the toilet

"At the campsite there is a stream to get water from." they say.

"There also is a river close by." they say.

I needed water desperately before ending my day and checked out my options. The stream they mentioned in the trail notes was a brown, sluggish, runny one, not quite inviting to drink from. I was not surprised of its conditions with all the moo-moos around. I had to go down to the river, which was easier said than done; the closest point to access the river was a sheer drop of 15 meters, there was no way I'd go down there and back up again. So, I had to walk and find another place that was accessible. With all my water bottles, I left the cows and my tent, and found a good spot for resupplying. Again, to a hiker's disgust the river was almost as bad as the little stream, only bigger and rather pee-yellow than poop-brown. Under painful attacks from sandflies I got my water filter out, to clean the yellow broth, and back at the tent I used some water purifying tablets to treat it and hopefully to kill the remaining bacteria.

It got dark and I was tired from the day. After dinner and with a few silent cow farts in the background I eventually fell asleep.

A loud rustling woke me up around 4am. I found my tent sides so close to my face, I could have almost inhaled them. The wind gusts that night were trying to break the tent poles, and I remembered Luca telling me about his night at this campsite here. He had experienced the same. On this grassy flat piece of paddock tents were exposed to the gusts without any protection. For two hours I fought with my hands and arms to not get blown away and tried to give my tent the best stability I could. Then I heard a cough! It was merely cow Nr. 723, standing close to the electronic fence, waiting for the result in the battle "man and tent vs gale-forced winds."

Telford Campsite is the compromise of the TA Trust with Mt Linton Station, the privately-owned farm, I had to cross the next day.

A sign advised hikers to not cross the fence after 4pm, just to make sure that people wouldn't walk over the farm in the night or even pitch their tents somewhere on the property. So, Mt Linton Station generously provided this little camp spot to use.

The 19 kilometers over Linton Station was just another iconic New Zealand farm, there were many, many "Baaaas" alias sheep in the beginning and many, many "Moooos" alias cows in the end.

The last kilometer to a road, I ended up hobbling and limping.

Two hunters had just come out of the bush and gave me a lift into Tuatapere or "Tui" and there I had the entire hostel to myself.

There are approximately six sheep per person in New Zealand! BAAA!

Oh Deer!

According to the two hunters in the car, it was the "Roar", it was hunting season in New Zealand. Everywhere, people got out into the bush now to shoot deer.

That was a great information to have and again something were I just couldn't make up my mind over what to do. I stayed in the hostel for another Zero Day and talked to locals about "The Roar".

"I wouldn't go into the Longwood Forest, I wouldn't trust the hunters' skills!" a woman in the supermarket told me.

"Oh, yea, you know, just last year the president of the hunting club, an experienced guy, aye, accidentally shot and killed another hunter, you know." a bloke added. Awesome! Now I had the choice between taking a forest full of seemingly unskilled hunters, or I would walk State Highway 99 into Colac Bay. Either or, it would take me two days to get there.

The problem was, I had gotten so fragile and tired. I didn't trust my body to last a long day in the woods anymore.

Neither, I wanted to just skip the section and walk on the easy road.

But then I didn't want to get shot in the forest either.

On the other side the tarseal on state highway would be more horrendous for my already sore feet.

U noticed? I carried on like I had done it on the North Island, with the decision of whether to leave my Trail Family or not. I had real decision anxiety and that got worse with my physical state of being that very moment. Whatever I would choose, I had to live with the outcome!

I took State Highway 99 the next day and felt unhappy and unsatisfied the whole time, until I reached the small town Orepuki and got a lift back to Tuatapere, 20 kilometers away.

"No, that was not what I wanted. That day was silly." I angrily growled.

I was disappointed with choosing state highway over the Longwood Forest. In anger and rage over the situation and the still remaining blister pain on the right foot, I took my pocket knife to eventually make a change!

Oh, I didn't hurt me, sorry. Instead I stabbed my right shoe and cut a big hole in the front side to release the pressure on the heel and toes.

"Now I will walk the forest tomorrow!" I told myself.

Trail Journal entry for Monday 18.4.16, Day 191
Wanted to go to the trail head of the Longwood Forest but all locals told me not to go in there because of the hunt.
Took state highway.
Hated it, depressed about decision, disappointed and demotivated.
Foot and blister terribly sore all the way. Waddled into Orepuki and hitched back to Tuatapere.
Bad mood! Sad! Don't know what to do!
Cut hole in right shoe to give toes and heel more room.
I want to walk the forest but not sure whether foot holds up and unsure with this hunting stuff going on. But unhappy with state highway at the same time.
I'm so confused. I think I will go into the forest tomorrow!

The next morning, I felt ready for the woods and got a lift to Merrivale, the start of the Longwood section. A local woman dropped me off, and before I closed the door she said "Oh girl, if I was your Mum, I would hate seeing you walking into a forest during the Roar. Please make sure you stay safe!" Yaaay! Just about when I thought I was ready and mentally prepared for it, this sentence quickly wiped my courage out in no time.
I still carried on, along deer fences and the walk was followed by the constant calls "Rrrrooooooaaaaaaaarrr." "Rrrrooooooooooaaaaarrr." "RRROOOOOOOOOOARRR!" I parroted the deer behind the fence.

A guy in a four-wheel drive saw me walking on the gravel road towards the forest and stopped for me. He decided to give me a lift further up, instantly took the wrong turn off, and we followed a forestry road in the opposite direction to where the track started.
That gave me the time to tell him about my little "Deer-Season-Issue."
He replied: "If you don't feel comfortable with it now, don't do it."
30 minutes later he dropped me off in Tuatapere.
State Highway 99 it was then!

I got a lift to Orepuki, the town I had turned around yesterday. It was just before lunch time when a muddy UTE rushed by, on the back a dead, bloody deer with one foot dangling out and waving at me.
"ROOOAARR" I yelled and started hammering my feet on the hard ground towards Colac Bay.

"ROOOOOAAAAAR!" he says

"Buuuuuuuuh!" I say

On my whole TA journey, I had been through almost everything one could think of, only one thing was missing: I hadn't been sick!
I jinxed myself and ended up with my face over the toilet in the night of the 20th of April. Yea, right! I had another Zero Day in Colac Bay!

Trail Journal entry for Wednesday, 20.4.16

Threw up around 4am. Haha, the TA really wants to make it hard for me, bugger that, sorry TA, I am too close to the finish line now.
Bloody life tests!
Ah well, had another Zero Day then and slept in campground's lounge, warm and dry there.

Happy Birthday René!

Came Thursday I only felt a little better, but I would only walk to Riverton, just a hop over the hill away. I saw dolphins playing in the water while walking on the beach and had the pleasure to park my butt on farmer Marc's quadbike, while he herded his sheep on his farm along the trail.
He dropped me off, I climbed the last official hill, entered the last official bush section and stopped at a lookout. I gazed over the long Oreti Beach ahead and tried to not focus on the landmass in the distance which was Bluff. Now it was definite, the trail had ended for René, Mike, Rick, Alba, Nathalie, Joel, Luca, Davorin, Gareth, Niko, Lucie and all the TA hikers I had met on my journey and my one would soon end, too!
There was no way I could avoid finishing it.

A day walker turned up on the lookout and noticed "You look like you've been on a long hike?" "Yes, it was." I replied.
We chatted about the TA and he talked about his soon to be finished New Zealand holiday. I guess we both were feeling melancholic!

I spent the afternoon and night in cosy, little Riverton and started off, the next morning, with a heavy heart, and walked towards Invercargill.
Oreti Beach was like 90 Mile Beach. The trail was like a circle. What had started on the top ended on the tip. I had continued on a beach and now I followed a beach towards the finish line. The penultimate day of the trail was like the second day in the beginning of Te Araroa Trail!

Yes, it almost was the same, except for now it was not the virgin start of an adventure, but the mature end!

The last official night on the TA in Invercargill was a sleepless one, like the first night on the TA had been, and in the morning, I got up to finish Te Araroa Trail.

Just a Day on the TA

Trail Journal entry for Saturday 23.4.16, Day 196

I leave the backpackers in the morning.
I feel complete.
Every move is perfect, my gear knows its place in the backpack, my feet know the way. Everything got perfected over the last months.
I start to walk and do what I have been doing for months, it is an uneasy feeling and I don't feel like smiling.

In my head plays a movie about memories of the first days on the trail. All the situations, all the people. They vanish, and other memories appear.

And then, it is the routine that keeps me walking, a permanent profound call to always step one foot ahead.

Only state highway and the people in their cars remind me of what lies ahead.
They cheer, wave at me and use their horns.
I feel proud and sad at the same time.

Bluff comes closer.
Would it be easier to just turn around and walk back to where I came from instead of carrying on?

I reach Foveaux Walkway. The big orange painted triangle shaped rock marks the last kilometers on Te Araroa Trail and I hold back the tears.

I've got one hour to go.
For the last time the trail makes me hate it. A soggy ground, mud holes, little streams, wet shoes and socks.

20 minutes to go.
I am not ready.
One step at a time.
I am scared of every corner I see.
I fear seeing Stirling Point.

And suddenly it is here and I realise that it is too late to turn around now, I am too close.

300 meters.

An elderly woman passes me.
She smiles "Congratulations" and seems amazed. I don't know how to react, I just feel like crying.

10 meters.
Five meters.
Breath.
One meter.
Done!
Roughly 3000 kilometers, just done!

It is 4:11pm on the 23rd of April 2016, it is a Saturday. It is stormy out on the sea, it had rained and then there are blue patches in the sky and a bit of sunshine.

I stand at Stirling Point and there is nothing!
My head is switched off, I am not happy. I am not sad. There are no emotions!
I take my pictures, gaze over the ocean and then leave.
Back to Invercargill.

I get out of the car and step on the footpath in front of the hostel.
I realise I have left something behind, I am not complete.
Something is missing.
A friend? The goal? The meaning?
I had finished Te Araroa Trail!
The adventure of a lifetime!
What a walk!

Stirling Point, Bluff

Stinky and I at the southern terminus of the TA

Epilogue

Reaching Bluff was just another moment on Te Araroa Trail; nothing special and so different from what I had expected it to be. The events to remember happened during the 195 days before arriving in Bluff. The trail was never meant to be about the destination but about what we fill the time with until we get there.

I got given the chance to fill my journey with amazing people, who turned into friends, and also to experience the TA in solitude. Neither of them I would want to miss. The people I met filled my heart and the solitude fed my horizon.

Still the emotions that didn't hit me in the moment of reaching Stirling Point, hit me the next hours and days afterwards. I had booked into the same hostel in Invercargill, returned there, hugged a Dutch TA hiker, who had finished the trail just a few minutes before I did, had a shower as usually after a long day's hike, and burst into tears under the warm water. It was like my heart got ripped into pieces and it felt like I just had buried my best friend, and nothing would bring him back.

I was not hungry and not tired anymore. Everything I had worked and planned for, all the tears and exhaustion, the joy, the struggle and love – It all had not prepared me for that day and I hadn't prepared for it.

I spent a week in Southland, stayed in the Riverton hostel, locked myself into a room and grieved over my friend, the trail. My body was shattered, and I was done with New Zealand. I was alone, had no idea of what to do with myself, and what I needed was a friend that knew how it was to finish a trail. I returned to Wellington and stayed at René's to let time go by.

Post-trail-depressions are common; you have had a purpose to get up for every day and were working towards achieving your goal by daily walking. All your focus laid on reaching the trail terminus. If I had known how hard those depressions can be, I would have tried to prepare myself for it, if at all possible to do so. I don't have a tip for how to deal with it, but just to let it be and accept your feelings about it. Mourn, distract yourself with stuff you enjoy, talk to fellow hikers, write a book, plan a new adventure, find a new goal, and give yourself time. Life always carries on, even after a journey like that.

For me, the really deep mourning process slowly disappeared after a few weeks, as life happened. But even two years from then, the feelings are vivid.

Going back to "real" life, to a job, to wardrobes, to cars and societal responsibilities was not easy and still is not.

I look at many things different now after having escaped the "rat race" once. My mind has changed over the time I have walked the trail, and my tolerance for many things in the 'real world' has alarmingly decreased.

Do I have to adapt and join in again? I don't think so, I don't want to!

The people I have met on the TA are now following their life trails, some are on adventures, some at universities and many back at work and "normal" life. Some people have had a longer lasting impact on me and remain present, but most of them have left homeward bound after finishing the TA – still we haven't left our lives.

I know that with all the hikers I have spent a decent time with, there will always be a deeper bond in us, even in years to come those people will be family, we are sharing the same marks, making it a "home" in everybody's hearts where ever we go.

While many people disappear "in persona" out of my daily life something that doesn't disappear are the daily up popping images and memories of the trail, the faces of the people, and the moments in the bush.

Even two years after finishing my adventure there is a profound yearning for the freedom I have experienced. I still feel the wind in my face, the sun on my skin, the water around my legs, (yes, the wet socks, too), I hear the birds in the trees and sense the rewarding feeling of making distance by foot.

I go through the pictures of my journey and I am back on Te Araroa Trail.

I write the book, clear memories come flashing up again and I am back on the TA.

There is no day where I do not think of it, the nature and the basic simple life. There is no day without Te Araroa Trail.

My gear is all set up in the shelf, the walking poles are extended to my size, and Stinky is ready to sit on my shoulders, to be carried over mountains, meadows and streams again.

How about an other adventure on a trail, somewhere in the world?

I am ready, *"the mountains are calling, and I must go..."*

Te Araroa Fun Facts

11.10.2015 – 23.04.2016	196 Days

Nr. of Days in motion (incl. canoeing)	128
Nr. of Zero Days	32
Nr. of Rest Days due to injuries	36
Nr. of rainy days	6
Best Zero Days	Mercer, Wellington

Most unproductive day	2hrs walk by Lake Pukaki

Nr. of nights in tent	69
Nr. of nights in beds	76
Nr. of nights in huts	35
Different sleeping places	16 (e.g.Tarp or Hobo Tin Hut)

Earliest get up	2am Lake Pukaki

Most favourite walks	Cape Reinga, Puketi Forest, Richmonds to Arrowtown
Most unpleasant walks	Te Kuiti to Pureora, Otira Flood Track

Hitchhikes (to trail, resupply, etc)	40
Falls	10
Lost toe nails	11
Nr. of hikers I met	83
Best cheat	Colac Bay, with farmer Marc

Showers on North Island	30+ 1 bath tub with a view
Showers on South Island	17
Longest stretch without shower	10 days
Average pee break/day	1

Best starry sky	Motatapus, Tekapo, Blue Lake
Worst sandfly spots	Pelorus River, Taramakau Mavora Lakes, Carloyn Bivvy

First hug	15.10.15
Last hug	23.04.16
Chocolate	9kg
Cheese	6,7kg
Peanuts	3,2kg
M&Ms	2,8kg
Snickers	47
Oats	6,7kg
Fish n Chips	10
Worst lunch	Peanut Butter & Honey (9 days)
Worst snack	Dried fruit and nuts (9 days)
Food I may never eat again	Couscous
Food I ran mad for	Bananas

Check out: **www.caminoteararoa.wordpress.com** for René's online blog!

Yes, please, find your own way of living!

Printed in Great Britain
by Amazon